Praise for Ric Vandett a

Hurdles – Surviving Difficult Times

"Much more than a self-help book, Dr. Ric Vandett's engaging book is part memoir and part manifesto. Frankly sharing his own personal hurdles -often challenging and sometimes humorous - Ric offers guidance that will be useful to anyone attempting to reconcile life's hurdles with their own core values. Reading this book is like sitting down over a cup of coffee with a new friend—and not wanting to finish the cup of coffee because you know there's so much more to learn about yourself just from listening to your new friend."—**Jane M. Everson, PhD**, University of South Carolina School of Medicine

"A paradigm-shifting narrative for navigating life's journey. Dr. Vandett's down-to-earth style of writing pivots his own rich life experience as an amazing guide for personal accountability and assessing your own perception lens.

As a former addict who clumsily tripped over hurdle after hurdle, I wish this book would have been available to me years ago. And now I assist homeless veterans find permanent housing. One of the first conversations I have with these veterans is around identifying barriers and developing strategies to overcome them. This book will be a perfect resource for my clients."—**Dallas Bragg, PhD**, Homeless Veterans Case Manager, Asheville Buncombe Community Christian Ministry (ABCCM)

"WOW! What an outstanding book. It is inspiring, motivational, and most importantly it is timely and beneficial to others facing some of the same hurdles in life.

Reading this book reminded me of the many young people that came from similar situations that Dr. Vandett describes. While thinking of them I wondered how many never went beyond "you are not college material." Ric's book serves as a beacon of hope for both youth and adults facing similar Challenges in their lives. Hurdles epitomizes, 'don't let the first step in your journey of life determine your future destiny.'

Awesome Read!"—**Steve O. Hunt**, Executive Director of the Office of Multicultural Affairs, Catawba Valley Community College

"Ric Vandett's book is a crash course on self-reflection and self-direction. His ability to write honestly about picking yourself up from the bottom of the pit and climbing up, held-head high, one rung at a time, is essential reading for today's often turbulent world. He addresses personal relationships, social media, religion, politics and substance abuse. These issues touch many of our lives, and from personal experience, Ric shares how it is possible to overcome the many hurdles that come our way."—**Hank Guess**, City of Hickory, North Carolina—Mayor

"If you have been lucky enough to meet Dr. Ric Vandett, you will instantly notice that he has a commanding presence, and yet he still devotes his full attention to those around him. He exudes belief in people's ability to not only meet but to exceed their goals. The more time you spend with him, the more you begin to believe in yourself. You realize that you have the intelligence, courage, and compassion to live up to your life's ambition. As a result, it came as no surprise to me that Dr. Vandett's book, *Hurdles*, would provide a message of how we have 'within us all we need to overcome obstacles, to reach our goals, to be happy.' Through the sharing of his life and his wisdom, *Hurdles* is a compelling, genuine, and wise set of instructions for living a life of meaning and compassion."—**Brice Melton**, Chief Academic Officer, Catawba Valley Community College

"A powerful and heartfelt journey through Dr. Ric Vandett's life. Through bold honesty, he reflects on challenges he has faced, sharing strategies to overcome difficult obstacles and for surviving personal tragedy. Through his experiences and faith, he enlightens us as to how to achieve the ultimate goal of leading a happy and fulfilling life while making a difference in the lives of others. This book truly motivates us to remove our hurdles or soar over them!"—**Tracy Hall**, Executive Director, Catawba Science Center

Other books from Redhawk Publications:

Birdhouse by Clayton Joe Young and Tim Peeler

The Bost-Burrus House: A Family Saga by G. Leroy Lail

Bouquets Hadn't Been Invented Yet by Tony Deal

Food Culture Recipes from the Henry River Mill Village

From Darkness: The Fated Soules Series, Book One by Jan Lindie

Going To Wings by Sandra Worsham

The Hickory Furniture Mart: A Landmark History by G. Leroy Lail and Richard Eller

Hickory: Then & Now by Richard Eller and Tammy Panther

Hickory: Then & Now The Complete History by Richard Eller

Hickory: Then & Now The Complete Photograph Collection

The Legends of Harper House - The Shuler Era by Richard Eller *More* by Shelby Stephenson

Mother Lover Child & Me by Erin Anthony

Newton: Then & Now by Richard Eller and Sylvia Kidd Ray

Piedmont The Jazz Rat Of Cunningham Park by Mike Bruner

A Place Where Trees had Names by Les Brown

Polio, Pitchforks & Perseverance by Richard Eller

Sanctuary Art Journal 2018, 2019, 2020

Secrets I'm Dying to Tell You by Terry Barr

Sittin' In with the Sun by Carter Monroe

Sleeping Through the Graveyard Shift by Al Maginnes

Waffle House Blues by Carter Monroe

We Might As Well Eat by Terry Barr

We See What We Want to See: The Henry River Mill Village in Poetry, Photography, and History by Clayton Joe Young and Tim Peeler

What Came to Me—Collected Columns Vol One by Arlene Neal

Win/Win by G. Leroy Lail

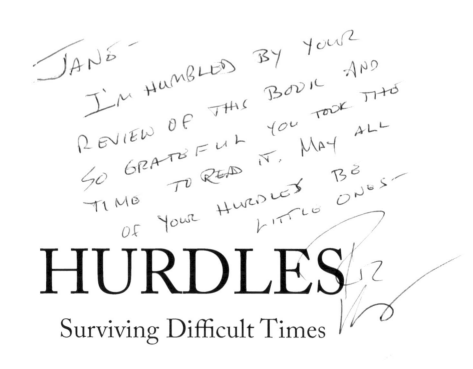

JANE —
I'M HUMBLED BY YOUR
REVIEW OF THIS BOOK AND
SO GRATEFUL YOU TOOK THE
TIME TO READ IT. MAY ALL
OF YOUR HURDLES BE
LITTLE ONES —

HURDLES

Surviving Difficult Times

Ric Vandett

Hurdles: Surviving Difficult Times

Published by
Redhawk Publications
2550 US Hwy 70 SE
Hickory NC 28602

Robert Canipe Editor-in-Chief and Publisher
Patricia Thompson Editor

ISBN: 978-1-952485-14-5

Table of Contents

Acknowledgments

The impetus for this book is the fond memories I have of teaching and coaching high school students. I have wonderful mental images of the many interactions and discussions I had with my students and players. I have to acknowledge that without those interactions I would never have thought about writing a book about helping people overcome obstacles in life.

Sadly, I have to acknowledge that our son, Matt, and his struggles played a major role in my wanting to put my thoughts on paper.

I also acknowledge the role played by many of my veteran friends with whom I interact often because I see the struggles many of them have, and I'm painfully aware that obstacles to success and happiness confront people of all ages and all walks of life.

Of course, I must acknowledge the contributions of my wife, Angela, who has experienced many of my personal hurdles and helped me overcome them. Without her, my life would have been more difficult and less fulfilling.

I want to dedicate this little book to all my former students and players, to the Foothills Veterans Helping Veterans in Hickory, NC, to my sons Vince, Dean, and Jared, all of whom my wife considers as her own, and, most especially, to my wife Angela. There is no hurdle I cannot overcome with you by my side.

Foreword

By Austin Pearce

Executive Director, Hickory Soup Kitchen

Life is like a baseball game. In this game we all play a different position. Not by choice or talent, but randomly. Let me explain... I'll put myself in it, helping explain.

I was born the son of a criminal defense attorney in an upper middle-class neighborhood, and grew up truly without need. Our power was never turned off, our fridge was always full, and I was made to feel like I was special and loved. It didn't come without life's challenges. A divorce, alcoholism, a child off course, trouble at school, trouble at work, even financial difficulties came my way. But the one constant was my father's ability to continue working. Our income never stopped flowing. So, in the game of life, I figure I was born on third base. Now, I didn't do anything to get to there. I didn't train to hit a ball, run, or catch anything. I just woke up one day, and I was already in the game.

Fast forward 43 years, and I'm doing well. I'm the Director of the Hickory Soup Kitchen. We serve hot, nutritious meals to our hungry on a daily basis. I have a beautiful, intelligent wife. A car, home, my health, and all that I need to live a full, enriched life. I've had family, coaches, and teammates cheering me on, teaching me, picking me up when I stumbled, and encouraging me to keep going. So, in the game of life, I'm headed to home plate.

Now, let's put David, one of our homeless guests at the Hickory Soup Kitchen, in the game. David was born on the same day and year as I, but he was born at, or below, the poverty line, which is not even inside the ballpark.

He has probably never seen the game played by anyone he knows. David grew up not knowing where his next meal may come from, or whether the electricity would be on at his home when he returned from school. He was discouraged at an early age by his parents and siblings from believing he would ever amount to anything. His mother told him once, "David, you will be a loser no matter how hard you try!" Walking to the bus each day for school, he was witness to poverty and desperation that he was assured by others would be his fate. There was no encouragement from family, friends, coaches, or teammates for David.

While both David and I had hurdles in life, it's clear that David had significantly more disadvantages. I had mentors that could help me assess and clear my hurdles. David did not. And this is where Ric Vandett's book, *Hurdles – Surviving Difficult Times*, enters. It's a playbook for the many people in our communities that simply never had the wherewithal to look at their life's obstacles as merely hurdles that one must overcome.

I've known Ric for over eleven years, as a volunteer at our soup kitchen as well as a volunteer with local veteran stand downs. As fellow Tar Heel fans, we became fast friends enjoying sports, politics, and service. Ric's mentorship and willingness to share his knowledge and leadership skills has helped me be successful in my own life. As I read his book, *Hurdles*, it became clear to me that once again, Ric is selflessly giving us all yet another gift. His book will help our community members who are ill-equipped to face life's seemingly unsurmountable challenges.

With his down-to-earth writing style, along with humor, grace and candor, Ric presents a reasonable approach to handling life's hurdles. Today, as I write this foreword to his captivating self-help guide I think we just might be able to get a few more folks into the ball game and up on the mound.

Ric, I thank you!

As often as you did it for one of my least brothers, you did it for me.

—Austin Pearce, March 2021

Introduction

These are difficult times. While we have made incredible advances in technology – most people on this planet are carrying a supercomputer and a high-tech camera (disguised as a phone) wherever they go – advances in human interaction and in personal self-confidence have not kept pace with the growth of technology.

Economic concerns – the rich get richer and many people still struggle to get from paycheck to paycheck (IF they have jobs at all!) – combined with an absence of human dignity in many cases as exemplified by the nastiness in political rhetoric, have enhanced people's feelings of helplessness, hopelessness, and depression.

"Life, liberty, and the pursuit of happiness" seem to be beyond the grasp of many people. While most have the goal of living a safe and secure life in which they can pursue happiness, many people find that there are obstacles or hurdles in their way.

These hurdles become barriers to the pursuit of happiness causing many to sink into the morass of helplessness, hopelessness, and depression.

When I was a high school teacher, I found myself talking to and counseling many young people on how to face some of life's difficulties. I often used analogies to help my students understand the points I was trying to make, and I have put some of those analogies along with my thoughts on how best to face and overcome the hurdles in the following pages.

What follows is not a scholarly treatise. Instead, it is the sharing of what I believe is a common sense approach to facing life's difficulties. My hope is that someone reading this may find something that will help him or her in the pursuit of happiness.

Chapter 1: Hurdles

Once upon a time I was a high school English teacher, and during a discussion of setting and achieving goals an image popped into my mind, and I shared it with my students. I asked them to look at reaching goals in life by comparing a one hundred meter dash to a one hundred meter hurdle race. I told them to consider the starting line as their current points in life. The finish line would represent whatever goals they had, e.g. an "A" in my class, a new car, getting accepted to college, just passing my class by the skin of their teeth (and why do we think teeth have skin?) finding a date for the prom, and so on.

Now if life were like a one hundred meter dash, I told them, then the only determining factor in achieving one's goal would be how fast that person chose to run. But life is not like a one hundred meter dash. Instead, it is more like a one hundred meter hurdle race: same starting point; same goal(s). But now there are obstacles in the way. Hurdles put there by others, by ourselves, by life's circumstances. And each hurdle, each obstacle, is something we must overcome if we are to reach our goals.

In all my years of teaching, actually in all the years I can remember of my life, I have known people who gave up when they faced that first obstacle. And they always had an excuse:

My teacher (parent, boss – fill in the blank) doesn't like me

Life is not fair

I wasn't given a fair chance

These classes are too hard

The list of excuses goes on and on. And they all have one thing in common: *It's always someone else's fault!*

The character of a person is determined by how he or she reacts to that first hurdle. Too many simply give up on their goals and on themselves. They wander aimlessly through life never setting goals because they have convinced themselves they could never attain their dreams.

But there are others who understand life is full of hurdles, and, when facing that first hurdle, they make every effort to overcome that hurdle. I shared with my students some of the hurdles I had experienced in life and how I was determined to get over each hurdle some way, somehow. I saw the movie *White Men Can't Jump*, so I knew I would have difficulty jumping over a hurdle. But the idea, seriously, is simply to overcome the hurdle by any means possible. Metaphorically that means jumping over it, climbing up and over it, going around it, or simply knocking that sucker down.

§

When I was twelve years old, my mother, my siblings, and I moved into a housing project in Youngstown, Ohio. We were on welfare, and I can vividly remember going to a warehouse downtown the first of each month to pick up our surplus food items. We got blocks of cheese, large cans of peanut butter that had oil on top that had to be mixed with the peanut butter on the bottom in order to make it edible, powdered eggs, powdered milk, flour, cornmeal, and an assortment of other items. Mom was a great cook, and she knew how to use these items to feed us good meals and how to make those items last an entire month.

We had cornbread almost every meal, and I was in my early 30's before I would eat cornbread again. I live in North Carolina now, so eating cornbread is some type of state requirement, I think.

But I didn't mind living in the projects. I had a lot of friends, and we all seemed to take our living circumstances in stride. I recall one of my first goals during that time. As my friends and I were walking to the junior high school about a mile and half away, we all decided to see how many "F's" we could get on our report cards. I was in the eighth grade at the time, and I had six subjects. I was hoping to fail all six classes. It was an attainable goal because most of the guys were six for six! I wasn't quite up (down?) to their level. I failed four classes. When my mother saw the report card, she told me that if I didn't get my grades up I'd be going to Catholic school after the second grading period. I had just spent two years in Catholic school before moving to the projects, and I did not want to go back – too strict for me. I actually received a great education in Catholic school, but at that time in my life I did not realize that. Mom pressure was stronger than peer pressure. I got my act together and changed my goals.

Peer pressure is powerful and often causes young people to make choices that bring about negative results. Thus, peer pressure is a hurdle that keeps people from attaining their goals. And peer pressure impacts folks of all ages, not just teenagers. While I did succumb to peer pressure (started smoking when I was thirteen), I decided to make an effort in school. I made good grades in junior high school and in high school. But in my senior year, when my mother and I met with the school Counselor, he told us that I was not college material. My mother was crushed. I didn't care much because I actually hated school. I accepted the lie that I would not succeed in college, and that was an example of not getting over a hurdle. When I made the bad choice to try and fail classes, I was essentially creating my own hurdle to successfully completing high school. And I allowed the counselor to erect a hurdle by accepting what he said.

A hurdle in achieving a goal is allowing other people's opinions of us to keep us from making the efforts needed to move forward.

Accepting that I did not have what it took to succeed in college forced me to take another road. College was not an option, I wasn't interested in going to work, and my mother was on my case to do something. The only option, then, was to join the armed forces. So I did. I wasn't interested in doing all the things that went along with joining the Army: sleeping in pup tents, eating out of mess kits, spending time in the field, taking care of a rifle, and so on. I joined the Air Force. After six months of training, the Air Force assigned me to the Army. I was trained as a weather observer, and wherever there were aircraft, there had to be a weather detachment. Fort Benning, Georgia, had an airstrip, so that is where I was sent. I spent two and a half years at Benning – spending a lot of time in the field on numerous operations, sleeping in pup tents, eating out of mess kits, and taking care of my weapons. I had outfoxed myself. Then, I went to Vietnam with the First Air Cavalry when the United States first began sending divisions in 1965.

So instead of going to college for four years following high school, I spent four years in the military. My life had taken a different path than my mother had hoped because I had allowed someone else to put a hurdle in my way (counselor saying I was not college material) and because I put a hurdle in my own way (not taking school seriously enough).

Hurdles get in the way when we put them there ourselves. Obviously, we put hurdles in our way by the choices we make. As I mentioned earlier, peer pressure is a powerful force that can cause people of all ages to make choices that put hurdles in the way of achieving goals.

The most insidious obstacles all fall under the heading of addiction. An addiction is simply that thing that is so important in your life that you can think of nothing else but feeding that addiction. Drugs, alcohol, smoking, and gambling are the obvious culprits, but people can also be addicted to porn, to binge eating and purging, sexual deviations, and, as in the case of Charles Manson and others like him, to serial murder. Whatever the addiction is, once hooked, a person has difficulties changing the behavior that is crippling that person.

> Hurdles get in the way when we put them there ourselves.

I can speak to the addiction of smoking first hand. I started smoking when I was thirteen and smoked on and off for twenty-one years. In August 1979, my wife, Angela, came home and told me she was pregnant. I quit smoking that day. She did as well, although when I was coaching high school basketball a few years later, she became so nervous during a triple overtime game that she had to go into the lobby to bum a cigarette to calm her nerves! When I smoked I never thought smoking could be an addiction. That belief was enhanced when I was able to quit cold-turkey (would love to know what "cold turkey" has to do with quitting something!). I figured if people wanted to quit they could. If I could, they could. I actually became – for want of a better term – a "born again" non-smoker. I had little patience with folks who said they just couldn't quit. Chief among those was my sister.

I have a picture of my sister Dianne when she was about three years old sitting in the front yard with a cigarette in her mouth. I'm sure the adults who posed her thought it was cute. Of course they had no way of knowing that smoking would kill her a week before her sixtieth birthday. She started smoking for real when she was sixteen. She developed health issues before she was forty, and just before her 50th birthday, she called to tell me she had COPD. I had heard of that disease but didn't really know how it affected one's body. She was scared because the doctor told her that if she didn't quit smoking she would be dead in 10 years. I remember getting very emotional and telling her she needed to quit smoking that day. But she didn't. Every time I tried to get her to quit she would say, "But I enjoy it so much." I could not convince her that it wasn't the smoking she enjoyed; it was her body's craving for the nicotine that was being satisfied. By then I understood that just because I was able to quit, that didn't mean she or anyone else who smoked could quit so easily. For some reason, my body did not get addicted to nicotine. I was lucky. My sister wasn't.

And I began to realize that addictions in many cases are diseases and need to be treated as such. People with alcohol and drug addictions are suffering from diseases, and in order to overcome the hurdles caused by their choosing drugs and alcohol, they must avail themselves of the "medicines" used to attack these diseases.

But once hooked, it is difficult for addicts to seek and stay on their "medicine." "Medicines" include, among other things, counseling, twelve step programs, actual prescribed medicines, peer support, and a variety of programs and experiences designed to help people change their behaviors. But medicine is no good if it is not taken.

Millions of families in this country have lost family and friends to alcohol and drug overdoses because the addicts simply refused help. We lost our youngest son due to his addiction to opioids. When he went to college he fell during a pickup basketball game and broke his wrist. He was prescribed an opioid, and his downhill slide began. Over the next eighteen years he see-sawed between sobriety and being under the influence of drugs. Detox and rehab worked for a while, and he tried to stay sober, but he didn't handle negative events well. He was able to help others through difficult times and was always there for others. He just couldn't help himself. He could not overcome the hurdle of addiction.

And that typifies what addicts go through. What no addict will believe is that he or she cannot overcome the hurdle alone. They understand there is a hurdle, but at some point that hurdle looks 100 feet high, insurmountable in their minds. And they give up. They give in to the demons of addiction.

Overcoming the hurdle of addiction takes a strong commitment from family and friends first to get the addict to admit there is a problem, and second to get the addict to commit to accept all the help that is available. Having someone to talk to in moments of weakness is essential if the hurdle is to be overcome. Those who won't admit and won't commit to help will lose more than not attaining their goals.

Chapter 2: The Pit and the Ladder

Once, in a conversation with someone who was upset, an image came to my mind. It was the image of a person standing in the bottom of a deep pit looking forlorn because he could not see a way out. His goal was to get to the top of the pit and thus get out, but the depth of the pit was, in his mind, too deep. His hurdle was insurmountable.

The pit represents that feeling of depression in which we feel powerless to overcome. When someone feels powerless, it becomes very easy to give up. Giving up causes the depression to worsen.

I remember teaching John Milton's *Paradise Lost*, and a line in that epic poem resonated with me and has stayed with me to this day. He wrote, "Hell is a place where there is no hope." Think of how many people see no hope in their lives. For them, life is "Hell on Earth." The addicts mentioned in Chapter 1 fall into this category. They are depressed, at the bottom of the pit, and they see no way out. They have no hope. They are in Hell. People who are that depressed know they are at the bottom of the pit, and they know where they want to be – at the top, out of the pit. But the depression is suffocating, and they see no way out of that pit. The top is just too far away.

In many discussions I have had with people, even my own son for whom it did not work, I have shared the thought that for every pit of depression there is a ladder of hope that provides a way out of the pit.

The key point about the ladder analogy is realizing that the focus of someone who is depressed should not be on the top of the pit, but, instead, the focus should be on the bottom rung of the ladder. The bottom rung of the ladder is attainable. Depending on the person, depending on the cause of the depression, the bottom rung of the ladder can be reached. People who care about others, who are trying to help friends and family members overcome their depression, should help identify what the bottom rung could be and, thus, begin to show how that rung could be reached.

For people of faith, that bottom rung could be God, Allah, Jesus, or any deity in whom someone believes. The 12-Step program for people trying to deal with alcoholism refers to this deity as a "Higher Power." For me, as a Christian, I try to get others to see that Christ could be that bottom rung. If "Hell is a place where there is no hope," then I share for Christians that "Hell is a place where there is no Jesus." Reaching the bottom rung is realizing that there is a power that could assist someone out of the pit of despair. If people truly believe in Jesus or another deity, they have reached the first rung.

Reaching the first rung should be a cause for celebration.

Once the first rung has been reached, the focus then changes to the next rung. Again, the situation and the people involved determine the nature of each rung, but it is essential to help people realize that each rung can be attained and that eventually reaching the top rung will bring people out of the pit and on steady ground.

For alcoholics, the 12-Step Program is a ladder designed to get them out of the pit of depression. That ladder has – well, 12 rungs.

My wife and I were familiar with the program because our son went through the first four steps when he was in rehab. Most people in rehab complete the first four rungs of the 12-step ladder while in therapy. Those who accept the program as their ladder continue on through the 12-step program. Upon completion, if they are not out of the pit, they are pretty darn close.

In extending the ladder analogy, it's important to realize that some ladders, especially metal ones, can often be slippery. Without diligence, without a focus on the goal, it's easy to slip on a rung and fall back. That's what often happens to people suffering from depression when a rung becomes difficult to attain. They lose focus and slip back. They relapse.

But addiction is not the only cause of depression. There are many causes. One is financial stress. Many years ago my wife and I were struggling financially. We had difficulty paying all of our bills each month. It always seemed that we ran out of money before we ran out of bills. I was the one who paid the bills, but I was not very organized. So, to get a handle on our situation, I wrote down all of the bills I knew we had to pay each month – mortgage, utilities, car payments, credit card payments, etc. Then I wrote down our combined take home pay and compared the two numbers. Ideally, the income should be much more than the outgo. And the difference between the two is the amount on which people could live each month (money for gas, food, clothes, etc.). When I looked at the numbers, I was stunned. The income barely exceeded the outgo leaving us virtually nothing on which to live for each month. I had resorted to letting some bills slide in order to buy the essentials we needed, and I had begun to depend on credit cards to help us get through each month, which, of course, made things worse.

Once I saw the numbers of our situation, I began a slow downward spiral into depression. I did not see a way out of the hole. Then we got the idea of selling our house. If we could get enough money from the sale of our house, we could pay our bills, and maybe pay off some of the bigger accounts (cars or credit cards). So we put the house on the market trying to sell it ourselves thus saving realtor's fees. We put a sign in the front yard and an ad in the newspaper. And we waited. And waited. Three weeks went by, and we never had anyone show any interest. Reluctantly, I took down the "for sale" sign.

It was February and very cold. To save on heating costs, we kept the furnace on low and used a fireplace insert to heat the modest ranch home in which we lived. One Saturday afternoon I had just finished splitting some logs that were in our backyard, and I cradled a load of wood in my arms preparing to take the wood to the house. I tried to walk but could not. While I had been splitting the wood I kept thinking about our situation. My solution – selling the house – wasn't working. That thought was on my mind when I stood up with the wood in my arms. But standing up was all I could do. I couldn't walk. I couldn't move. I was literally paralyzed with fear. At that time in my life I had not yet come up with the pit and ladder analogy, so I was not consciously thinking about trying to reach the bottom rung. But, in essence, that is exactly what I did.

> For every pit of depression there is a ladder of hope.

As I stood frozen to the spot, I looked to the sky and said, "Dear God, please help me. I can't do this alone. I give my life to you." I was very sincere when I said that I was putting my life in God's hands. At that moment a sense of peace and calm came over me, and I easily walked to the house. I shared the experience I just had with Angela, and I told her that someway, somehow, we would make it. I didn't know how, but I was confident we would be all right.

Two days later there was a knock on our front door. A man I had never met was standing there, and he asked if our house was still for sale.

The man told us he had driven through the neighborhood a couple of weeks earlier looking for a home for his parents. He made note of the sign in our yard as he looked in other neighborhoods. After searching for a couple of weeks, he decided that our house was the one he wanted. When he drove to our house and did not see the sign (he told us), he was disappointed. He thought about leaving but decided to check to see if we had sold the house. He was elated when he found that we still wanted to sell the house.

But this story took an interesting twist.

Once we agreed on a sale price, we had to have the house inspected. A friend of ours who worked for a heating and air company agreed to inspect our furnace which was located in the crawl space beneath the house. When he emerged from the crawl space, he had a strange look on his face. He told us there was a hole in the furnace and that it could catch on fire at any time. He was surprised that it had not already done so. He said we had to turn it off immediately. It was February and cold, and we didn't use the fireplace insert during the night. But we turned off the furnace. I called my folks who lent us the money for a new furnace, and we were able to sell the house. We made enough money on the sale to pay off the major bills and put down enough money to buy a new house.

It didn't take me long to realize that shortly after putting my life totally in God's hands He changed and saved , yes "saved," our lives. Had the man not come to the house asking if we still wanted to sell, we may not have sold the house. Thus, there would have been no reason to inspect the furnace, and we would have had no way of knowing the dangerous situation we were in. It is quite likely that the furnace would have exploded which could have killed us.

I'm not saying that God works so quickly and decisively in people's lives. It's quite possible that God had nothing to do with what happened in our lives, but the inner peace I felt when I turned to Him was real, and I was confident we would be all right. And we were.

As I look back at what happened so many years ago, I realize we reached the first rung out of the pit of despair and depression. I have since become extremely organized with our finances and can track and manage all of our expenses. Each stage of organizing our finances has been another rung in the ladder that we climbed to get out of the financial pit of depression.

Losing loved ones also causes depression, and it's a deep pit from which many people are unable to escape. Sadly, we learned that fact after we lost our son. I had no idea how many people we knew had lost a child. So many of our friends who expressed their condolences had also lost children, and we learned that each family, each person handles such a loss differently.

One such person mentioned that she understood our grief because her son had been dead for – and she listed the number of years, months, and days he had been gone. It appeared to me that her grief was all-consuming; it was all she thought about. I have since learned that her depression is serious, and she can't seem to get out of that pit of despair.

I told Angela that we would grieve and miss our son terribly, but that his loss could not consume our lives. We could not allow one loss to become three.

People who are depressed due to the loss of a loved one, especially a child, need to identify not only the bottom rung but the ladder itself. For many, that ladder could be the "Seven Stages of Grief," and each stage could be a rung on the ladder. Reaching the seventh stage would put a person near the top of the pit.

The Seven Stages of Grief

1. **SHOCK & DENIAL-**
   You will probably react to learning of the loss with
   numbed disbelief. You may deny the reality of the loss
   at some level, in order to avoid the pain. Shock provides
   emotional protection from being overwhelmed all at once.
   This may last for weeks.

2. **PAIN & GUILT-**
   As the shock wears off, it is replaced with the suffering of
   unbelievable pain. Although excruciating and almost unbearable, it is important that you experience the pain fully,
   and not hide it, avoid it or escape from it with alcohol or
   drugs.

   You may have guilty feelings or remorse over things you
   did or didn't do with your loved one. Life feels chaotic
   and scary during this phase.

3. **ANGER & BARGAINING-**
   Frustration gives way to anger, and you may lash out and
   lay unwarranted blame for the death on someone else.
   Please try to control this, as permanent damage to your
   relationships may result. This is a time for the release of
   bottled up emotion.

   You may rail against fate, questioning "Why me?" You
   may also try to bargain in vain with the powers that be for
   a way out of your despair ("I will never drink again if you
   just bring him back")

4. **DEPRESSION, REFLECTION, LONELINESS-**
   Just when your friends may think you should be getting
   on with your life, a long period of sad reflection will likely
   overtake you. This is a normal stage of grief, so do not be
   "talked out of it" by well-meaning outsiders. Encouragement from others is not helpful to you during this stage of
   grieving.

   During this time, you finally realize the true magnitude of
   your loss, and it depresses you. You may isolate yourself on

purpose, reflect on things you did with your lost one, and focus on memories of the past. You may sense feelings of emptiness or despair.

5. **THE UPWARD TURN-**
   As you start to adjust to life without your dear one, your life becomes a little calmer and more organized. Your physical symptoms lessen, and your "depression" begins to lift slightly.

6. **RECONSTRUCTION & WORKING THROUGH-**
   As you become more functional, your mind starts working again, and you will find yourself seeking realistic solutions to problems posed by life without your loved one. You will start to work on practical and financial problems and reconstructing yourself and your life without him or her.

7. **ACCEPTANCE & HOPE-**
   During this, the last of the seven stages in this grief model, you learn to accept and deal with the reality of your situation. Acceptance does not necessarily mean instant happiness. Given the pain and turmoil you have experienced, you can never return to the carefree, untroubled YOU that existed before this tragedy. But you will find a way forward.

The above model was taken from a number of online sources, and it is an extension of the popular Kubler-Ross model of the "Five Stages of Grief."

Each of the stages could be a rung on the ladder leading out of the pit of depression. It is important to note that not everyone handles grief the same way. But to understand the concept of the ladder and of each stage of grief being a rung on the ladder could help people deal with loss because it gives one a focus. All too often a person's focus is on the loss, and he never gets past the shock and denial stage. That stage only becomes a rung on the ladder when folks realize that shock and denial are normal reactions and accept that they must experience these emotions before they can get to the next rung.

My wife and I have gone through most of the stages. I can only speak for myself, but I see me as somewhere between the sixth and seventh stages. I'm "working through" and getting closer to "acceptance," but I'm not there yet. And there were times that I actually went down a rung or two. Just as my life would become a little calmer (stage 5), I would slip back into realizing the depth of my loss (stage 4) and even experience anger towards our son (stage 3). But I understand the ladder. I believe in the ladder, and I have accepted the stages of grief as rungs on that ladder.

And that belief is essential if we are to get out of the pit of depression. We can only get out of that pit if we truly believe there is a way out. The ladder analogy works for me, and I think it's a simple way for people to visualize a way out of depression.

Another thing that is important is to try to identify what the "top of the pit" is. I have used examples of depression caused by the loss of a loved one or by financial problems, but a hurdle to overcoming depression is not being able to pinpoint the cause of the depression.

I have a good friend who has been battling depression for a number of years, and he often cites his being suddenly fired from a job that he loved. There had been no warning. He went to work one morning only to be told his position was being eliminated. He was crushed, and his self-esteem plummeted. He is a smart man with a good heart and often counsels others, but every once in a while as he is trying to help someone he mentions getting fired from his job. It's obvious that incident has negatively impacted his life. If he were to embrace the concept of the pit and the ladder, he might realize that his depression is directly related to losing his job. He could look at the top of the pit and ask himself, "How best can I deal with being fired so that it doesn't drag me down?"

Recently I have become acutely aware of another cause of depression, and it is something I never considered. Retirement. I never thought that retirement could be a source of depression because when I retired, like many others, I was busier than when I worked for a living. But many retired people become depressed when they find themselves not as active as they once were. There are many options for retirees to keep themselves active and relevant, but many are unsure how to avail themselves of those options. It's important for friends and family to recognize that for some people, retirement is not all fun and leisure. It's important to look for signs of depression in our retired friends and family and to look for ways to help them out of their respective pits of depression.

There are many causes of depression and many ways to deal with it. But a person must first want to deal with it and believe he can be successful. One way to do that is to embrace the "Pit and Ladder" analogy. Depression is a major hurdle in people's lives, and the "ladder" can help them over that hurdle.

Chapter 3: The Cake and the Icing

I remember once trying to console a distraught teenager whose boyfriend had just broken up with her. I remember her words, "He was my life. He was all I cared about. He was my reason for living."

My reason for living. That got me to thinking. "If your reason for living is gone, why go on living?" It bothered me that young people often saw their reasons for living were other people, usually boyfriends, although I did counsel a few football players who were crushed when their girlfriends left them.

There is no reason not to be upset when relationships break up. Teenagers go through a lot of angst when they breakup, and adults often experience difficult times going through divorces. Hurt feelings, feelings of inadequacy, fear, and panic are just a few emotions people go through when relationships end. Those feelings are normal. They happen to us all. But the belief that another person is a reason for living is actually a hurdle that gets in the way of people living their lives to the fullest.

When other people are our "reason for living," it means we place more importance on other people than we do on ourselves. People's first reaction to that comment is that we should always think of others first; we should always put others before us. I'm sure I'm in the minority when I say, "That's the wrong way to look at life and relationships." I believe we need to take care of ourselves first.

Have you ever been on a plane? Just as you are getting in your seat, the flight attendant begins the speech, which most of us tune out, about safety features on the plane. The attendant usually ends with a demonstration of what to do if cabin pressure fails. The oxygen masks are released and adults are told, "Put yours on first. Then help someone else." In other words, take care of yourself first before helping others.

One way to help is by giving of ourselves.

We need to give of ourselves in order to make relationships work, but it's difficult to give of yourself if you are depressed or have a low self-image.

That brings me to the Cake and Icing. My reason for living should be to become a better me and to make a positive difference in the lives of other people. In essence, I am the cake. Everything else in life, the things that make life better, especially a successful relationship, becomes the icing. I can live without the icing, but not without the cake. I am the cake. But the icing just makes everything so much better.

I know many people have a goal of getting married. One problem with that thought is that once people are married, they have reached their goal. Then what? All too often the things people did to have a successful relationship while dating are forgotten once they are married. I believe the actual goal should be a successful relationship of which marriage is a part. Thus, getting married is a step towards the goal, but it is not an end in itself. If the goal is a successful relationship, then folks should focus on the things that make relationships successful. Successful relationships are based on mutual giving, and both people must feel good about themselves before they can truly give of themselves to others.

Since I'm using analogies, 1 want to share one about a rubber band and how it relates to making relationships successful. It also relates to my comment about taking care of oneself first.

I believe there needs to be a great deal of giving to make a relationship work. When a person gives of himself it's like extending a rubber band string to his partner. When the partner returns the giving, the partner is extending another band back to his/her partner. The constant giving to each other, extending the rubber bands back and forth, back and forth, back and forth many times strengthens the rubber band or bond between the two. The stronger the band (bond), the better it is able to withstand the things that break bonds, that cause relationships to break apart. The more giving there is, the stronger the bond.

Relationships fail when the bonds are weak. Giving on the part of one person and not the other causes the rubber band to be extended only one way. It is not being reinforced. Thus, when something happens to push against the bond, the band breaks, and the relationship suffers.

There are many things that can threaten a relationship. In no particular order – trust, poor communication, financial issues, infidelity, self-centeredness, self-doubt, and various addictions are some of the hurdles that threaten relationships. Even the strongest relationships are challenged by these issues, and only those relationships in which strong bonds have been firmly established can withstand the pressures created by the issues listed (and there are many other issues).

Trust – Trust is a two-way commitment. Trust is built up over time, not overnight. Trust is also the result of giving to each other strengthening the bond between two people. But if trust is not firmly established, or if something happens to cause one person to lose trust, a relationship suffers.

Poor communication – Nothing negatively impacts a relationship faster than poor communication. The first obstacle or hurdle in poor communication is assuming other people know what we are thinking or we know what others are thinking. Arguments often get started when one person asks "What's wrong?" and the answer is, "Nothing."

"Nothing" usually means "something!" But the person who says "nothing" often assumes that the other person really knows what the problem is and is waiting for that person to apologize for something about which the first person (are you still with me?) may not even be aware. If someone hurts us, we often shut down, clam up, or pout and keep things in. Not sharing what is bothering a person is a major cause of poor communication.

In Scripture, Jesus shares what we should do when we feel that someone has wronged us. In Matthew 18:15, Jesus says, "If your brother or sister sins, go and point out their fault, just between the two of you." In other words, if you feel hurt by what someone has said or done (or what you THINK someone has said or done), you should go to that person and talk. Share why you feel hurt. But all too often, we keep things inside and do not communicate. I'll share more about this concept in Chapter 7.

Keeping things inside and not communicating causes what is inside of us to fester. Think of a tea kettle (another analogy!). What happens when the water in a tea kettle begins to boil? The tea kettle whistles. What causes the whistle? It is literally "letting off steam." It is important for us to "let off steam" and not to keep things inside and let them fester. Think what would happen to the tea kettle if it did not have an outlet. We are no different. We need outlets, and communicating is an important outlet. Good communication begins when we understand the importance of talking to one another.

Financial issues – I have already shared our personal example of our financial crisis that happened many years ago, so I won't dwell on this issue. But it is important to understand that stresses due to financial problems are major hurdles to successful relationships. All too often things get out of hand, and couples do not talk about how to overcome the hurdle. They either don't discuss it (poor communication) or they assign blame for the problem and argue about who and what are to blame. As with any hurdle, the only way to overcome it is to face it. Deal with facts first. Ask the important questions. What is the actual income? On what is money being spent? What kind of changes need to be made to improve the situation? Using data and developing a plan while openly communicating with each other will help people overcome the financial issues hurdle.

Self-centeredness – A major hurdle to a successful relationship is the belief that the world centers around you. Self-centeredness should not be confused with selfishness. I mentioned earlier that being selfish is not a negative term (at least not how I define that word) because if means strengthening yourself to take care of others. Self-centeredness means strengthening yourself to boost yourself over others. A person who makes decisions solely on how it benefits him or her is creating his or her own hurdle to successful relationships.

Self- doubt – The opposite of being self-centered is being riddled with self-doubt. A poor self-image is a major hurdle to a successful life. If you think you cannot succeed, you will not. If you allow past failures to cause you to give up, you will create an almost insurmountable hurdle because you will never believe you can succeed. When asked about his innumerable failures while trying to invent things, Thomas Edison once said, "I have not failed. I just found 1,000 things that do not work."

I can speak to self-doubt because that was part of my personality growing up. Living in the projects and realizing how others saw me caused some self-doubt. Being told I was not college material added to that self-doubt.

> It is essential for all people to have dreams if we want to be successful, if we want to overcome hurdles.

After four years in the military, I went to work for an auto parts store in Freeport, NY. I had no goals of what I could become because I had no faith in myself. I left that store and went to work for the Post Office during the last three months of 1966. Delivering the mail was an easy job, and after a few weeks, I began to realize that I really wanted more of a challenge. I wanted more. My self-image was a little better, but I had a long way to go.

In January of 1967, a friend of mine whom I met in Vietnam called from his home in Buffalo, NY, and asked me to go to California with him. Four months earlier we were both discharged at the same time at Fort Ord in Oakland and enjoyed a couple of weeks in Los Angeles before going to our respective homes. There was just something about living in California that appealed to me, so I agreed.

I started going to Los Angeles Valley College for the spring semester and discovered a new me. My experience in the military, especially in Vietnam, matured me, and I approached school with a little bit of confidence. I remember telling one of the teachers that he used a "poor analogy," and he agreed with me. The other students were amazed that I questioned the teacher, but it just came naturally to me.

Later that year I got married, and we had a child, so I had to quit school and go to work. While I was working as a manager of a finance company, I began taking broadcasting classes at night in Hollywood. Eventually, we moved back to NY and had a second child. I went back to work for the post office but kept alive my dream – and let me stop here to emphasize the word "dream." It is essential for all people to have dreams if we want to be successful, if we want to overcome hurdles. Back to the dream – I wanted to keep alive my dream of working in radio, of becoming a disc jockey.

And the dream came true. In September of 1971 I was hired as a disc jockey at a small radio station in Wilkesboro, NC. I used the on air name of Ric Ross, and in a few short months, I was known to thousands (well, maybe hundreds) of people in Wilkes County. The four years I worked in radio enhanced my self-image, and that self-image was strengthened by my successful completion of an AA degree from Wilkes Community College and a BA in English from Appalachian State University, all while still working at the radio station.

A comment from a friend of mine really made a difference in my decision to go to App State. When I graduated from the community college, he asked me if I was planning to go to ASU. I said, "No." He asked why not. I said, "Man, I'm 28 years old. If I go to school in two years when I graduate, I'll be 30!" For some reason that sounded too old to graduate from school. He looked at me and said," Well, how old will you be in two years if you don't go to school?" I just stared at him and realized he was right. Sometimes things people say to us or do for us are aids in overcoming hurdles, and my friend's words were a catalyst for me. After graduation from ASU I took a job as a high school English teacher and a coach.

Before I retired from the public schools in 2009, I had earned a master's degree and a doctorate. The positive self-image I had from early successes in school in Los Angeles and in NC and that I derived from being a disc jockey helped set the foundation for the successes I achieved over the years. My positive self-image helped me overcome many hurdles.

Infidelity and addictions – I have already talked about how addictions impact relationships. Spouses and other family members suffer greatly when dealing with someone who has an addiction.

Infidelity obviously can have a negative impact on a relationship and is a hurdle that is difficult to overcome. I refer back to the analogy of the rubber band. A strong bond formed by giving of each other to each other can withstand even the betrayal of infidelity. But a weak bond cannot. When faced with the issue of infidelity, a couple must communicate all feelings – hurt, self-centeredness, self-doubt, anger, pride, etc. – and decide just how important the relationship is. Honest communication through the issue of infidelity could save a relationship worth saving.

A successful relationship is the goal, the cake if you will, and all the good things that go with a successful relationship become the icing on the cake. It takes work to make a relationship work, but it is usually worth every ounce of energy we put into it.

Chapter 4: The Wall of Security

None of us wants to be hurt. We want to be safe and secure – free from all hurt and pain. So we protect ourselves. I've always loved the character Linus in the "Peanuts" comic strip. As long as he had his blanket – his security blanket – he was all right. He was safe. Security blankets are pretty neat. They keep us safe and secure. But they can also keep us insulated from life. While we are wrapped up protecting ourselves, we are often keeping ourselves from experiencing life, both its ups and downs.

The more we get hurt, the more we want to protect ourselves from being hurt again. We often create a wall around ourselves insuring that no one could penetrate that wall and hurt us again. But there is a problem with a wall. It may keep things out, but it also prevents us from reaching out. And when we can't reach out, we become more wrapped up in ourselves.

Life is meant to be lived. That's a fairly trite saying, but it's true. I remember writing a poem once inspired by a movie Angela and I were watching at her apartment when we were dating. The movie was *The Way We Were* staring Barbra Streisand and Robert Redford. There was a scene in the movie of one of them (I can't remember who) sitting in a taxicab that was stuck in traffic. At that point an image came to me of being stuck in a motionless cab, and the words "the meter is running, and I am going nowhere" popped into my head. As I sat in the cab, I could see people walking five miles an hour into a ten mile wind struggling just to make it in life. So I wrote,

The Meter is Running

The road is crowded this rainy night

And city sounds and gusty howls

Are all I hear as I sit in

This motionless cab and watch the meter run

The meter is running

And I am going nowhere

I can see people over-protecting

Themselves against the elements

Walking five miles an hour into a

Ten mile an hour wind, and I can see that

The meter is running

And I am going nowhere

I can see the red light stopping

Cars and buses and cabs and

Causing people to shout and cuss and

Fight, and I can see that

The meter is running

And I am going nowhere

How insane it is to waste

A moment of a lifetime that lasts

But a Moment. How insane it is

To awaken to find that

The meter is running

And I am going nowhere

I have but one choice: to leave the cab and go with the wind; to love and live and touch and give, to never again say of my life that the meter is running and I am going nowhere.

I was determined then – and still am – to live life to its fullest, to open myself to what life offers rather than protect myself against whatever hurts life has in store. I know I am going to be hurt; I've been hurt a few times, a couple of which almost beat me down. But I refuse to stay down, and I have lived my life with the thought that since there are hurts I will simply live life as best I can between the hurts. And if the next hurt never comes, I'm just that much further ahead. One of my favorite lines in the poem is "How insane it is to waste a moment of a lifetime that lasts but a moment." It is so easy to forget that life is fleeting, and how important it is to live life to its fullest. I don't intend to waste moments.

In his poem "Mending Wall," Robert Frost wrote, "Something there is that doesn't love a wall ..." A wall is a barrier, an actual barrier that separates and doesn't allow for making positive connections. In essence, a wall is a hurdle that keeps people from enjoying life and living life to its fullest.

> "The meter is running, and I am going nowhere."

There are those who would argue that walls keep out the undesirables. Perhaps. But who are the "undesirables?" Walls segregate us, and segregation has proven to be a barrier toward personal growth. They prevent us from reaching out, from getting to know others. That's why, intrinsically, for many of us, "... there is something that doesn't love a wall."

We will never live life to its fullest if we feel we need walls to protect us. Another way to look at the wall is not that it represents safety. Instead, it represents captivity. To truly live and enjoy life, we must first admit that walls are barriers to enjoying life. The next step is to identify the specific wall that is the hurdle. Then either through one's own wits or with the help of others, we need to develop strategies to bring down the walls.

Life "lasts but a moment" and is too short to spend it protecting ourselves from the troubles life often throws at us. Building walls around ourselves does not offer us security. True security comes from within, from a strong sense of self-worth and self-confidence. That self-confidence will help us knock down the walls of insecurity which, in turn, helps us overcome hurdles in our lives.

Chapter 5: Crutches

Crutches are helpful. A few years ago I had major surgery on my leg. I had slipped on a patch of wet grass and ruptured my quadriceps. All the muscles, tendons, and nerves completely detached from my knee. Following the surgery, I wore a leg brace to keep from bending my leg, and I used crutches to move around as soon as I was able. Without the crutches I would not have been able to get from one place to another. I needed the crutches, as it were, to stand on my own two feet.

And that's what crutches are meant to do – to help people stand on their own two feet. But crutches were never meant to be permanent. A person with a broken leg or sprained ankle who doesn't give up the crutches because he or she feels secure with the crutches will rarely walk normally. People often fear that giving up the crutches too soon would be a mistake, so they come to rely on the crutch rather than work to heal the injury.

That fear of giving up the crutch on which someone depends is what keeps many people from healing their inner wounds. Thus, the crutch becomes a hurdle toward overcoming their problems.

For most drug addicts, the drugs become the crutches that instead of helping an issue actually can be fatally harmful. Many addicts start off innocently enough taking pills for pain.

While it is difficult to share this, the story of losing our son to a drug overdose is a prime example of allowing the crutch to become an insurmountable hurdle.

While he was in college, Matt broke his arm playing basketball. He had to have a pin inserted in his wrist, and he was put on painkillers – OxyContin. At that time my wife and

I didn't know about the painkillers. A lesson for all parents to learn is to find out right away the type of painkillers a child has been prescribed and what the possible side effects could be. Maybe, just maybe, if we had known the extent of what he was taking and the effect it could have on him, we might have been more proactive in treating the pain associated with the surgery to repair his arm. Maybe.

Over time we learned – through many heartbreaking incidents – that he was becoming hooked. He needed the crutch of the painkilling drugs so much that he began spending money we gave him for school on the pills. Then he got behind on what he owed his dealer. I bailed him out. Two years later it happened again. I bailed him out again. I was becoming the poster boy for enabling. I didn't realize until it was too late that instead of helping him overcome his hurdle, I was helping him maintain his crutch.

He never got rid of the crutch. At times he would stay clean for long periods of time, but subconsciously he believed that the drugs would handle any pain. He was no longer hurting physically. But whenever something caused him to be depressed, he dealt with that pain by relying on pills. He did have many highs. He graduated from Catawba Valley Community College and was accepted at Lenoir-Rhyne University. He found a woman who was a single parent with a newborn son, and Matt loved them both. But he just could not or would not give up drugs for any length of time. His drug use caused him to lose the girl and her son, a child whom Matt really loved. And the loss of that relationship caused him to spiral into a deep depression.

We were aware that he was struggling, but we believed something else was going on. We never found out what it was. We lost him to an overdose, and that loss as well as our frustration that we couldn't save our son has become a hurdle for Angela and me as we try to reach our goal of being happy.

Matt's story is not unique. His story has been and is being repeated hundreds of times daily. There are too many people whose drug addiction is a crutch of which they cannot let go and a hurdle they are unable to overcome.

But drugs are not the only crutch. Equally as insidious as drugs is alcohol. Let me give this disclaimer first – I drink. That sounds as though I drink a lot. I don't. But I like an occasional beer, I love red wine – mostly super Tuscans – and Amaretto over ice is a nice way to watch a romantic movie with my wife. But I will never be accused of being an alcoholic. I think the last time I was drunk was in 1967 when my friend Tracy and I were at the Golden Pagoda restaurant in Los Angeles' Chinatown. There was a piano bar, there was beer, there was music, I was singing, and the next thing I remember was waking up in our apartment in the San Fernando Valley. Tracy swore I drove home, but I have no recollection. Don't think I ever got that drunk again.

I'll have a beer occasionally, but usually not more than one. But I know, we all know, many people who could never stop at just one. Those who drink to excess do so, not because they love the taste of beer, wine, whiskey, etc., but because the alcohol, at least in their minds, is helping them cope with their problems. They believe the alcohol helps them face their hurdles.

As with a dependency on drugs, a dependency on alcohol makes the hurdle almost seem insurmountable, which causes the person to drink, which causes him to see his problems as unsurmountable, which causes him to drink, which causes . . .

Alcoholics Anonymous (AA) and Narcotics Anonymous (NA) are two programs designed to help people overcome their dependencies. These are good programs that have helped many people. I think there is a lot of merit to the

12-Step Program, but these programs often fail as many people as they help. Both programs try to delve into the causes of dependency, and both programs have a spiritual component to them. I am a firm believer in God and in the power of prayer. But each person who has succumbed to a dependency on drugs or alcohol has had people praying for him or her. It wasn't enough.

> Crutches were never meant to be permanent.

Obviously, you cannot help someone who is an alcoholic deal with his demons without getting him to deal with the drinking in the first place. Somehow, some way, the alcoholic must be made aware that the drinking is only making the hurdle more insurmountable. Programs such as AA and NA can help; counseling can help; tough love can help; interventions might help. But the key component is to care, to love, and to never give up. Our own lives are an example of that not being enough, but for many people, those activities may just be what they need to overcome their hurdles.

Another crutch is a dependency on other people to help us through life. We have all either known or heard about someone staying in an abusive relationship. Most of us never understand why the abused person doesn't just leave and get out of the relationship.

But abused people stay in the relationships because they have no self-confidence and don't believe they can make it on their own. Their "cake" is the abuser, and, to them, an abusive relationship is preferable to being alone.

Unless and until people can find the strength and courage to get out of an abusive relationship, they will continue to depend on other people to at least get through life. That dependency is a crutch that is a hurdle to success.

Helping people realize that a dependency on alcohol, drugs, tobacco, other people, or any obsession that someone feels is helpful are actually crutches that do not help in the long run. To stand on one's two feet, to be independent, we all have to cast aside our crutches.

Chapter 6: Anchors

Anchors can be stabilizing forces, and in many cases that is a positive aspect of anchors. The image of a boat anchored in the bay while folks are partying into the night would indicate anchors are pretty cool. People are having a good time, the boat is secure, and all's right with the world.

As long as we want our boat to stay motionless, we are satisfied with our anchor. But what happens if we want to move? Unless we make an effort to bring up the anchor, we are going nowhere.

One of the popular phrases of introspective people from the 1960's and 1970's was, "I don't know who I am." That mantra allowed people to meander through life searching for "who they were." I believed then as I do now, that we often ask the wrong questions. People who were not satisfied with themselves or where they were in their lives asked the question, "Who am I?" as though the answer to that question would suddenly give them a sense of identity. The proper question to ask would have been (and still is), "What do I need to do to be happy, content, and/or satisfied with where I am in my life?" It's difficult to find an answer to who a person is. It's more constructive to seek out the things that would help someone be satisfied with his or her life.

Hurdles appear when we ask the wrong questions. If we are seeking to "find ourselves" and have difficulty doing so, we begin to create our own hurdles to success. Asking the wrong questions anchors us to a spot from which we cannot move because there is no answer to the question "Who am I?" that will help us move in a positive direction. Instead, searching for and identifying the things that could bring happiness and peace of mind are positive steps, and steps get us moving. And moving means we are no longer anchored.

When I hear the Navy hymn "Anchors Aweigh," I think of the word "weigh." Anchors weigh so much, and things that weigh on our minds can anchor us to the point that we don't feel as though we are making any progress in life.

When I was 19 years old I was stationed at Ft. Benning, GA, and I met a young lady who lived in Blakely, about 20 miles south of Columbus, GA. I went to visit her one weekend, and apparently something was bothering me a great deal. It must have seemed to her father that I was carrying the weight of the world on my shoulders. I cannot remember what I was worrying about, but I'll never forget her father's words. He said, "Son, how many problems have you ever solved by worrying about them?" That one statement/question has stayed with me all my life, and "Never worrying about things over which you have no control" has been a core belief of mine. If I can't control it, I don't worry about it.

Worrying about things we cannot control anchors us. We worry and worry and worry, and we accomplish nothing. If we know we cannot control whatever issue may be bothering us, then we either ignore the issue (if possible), or we identify the issue and think of ways to address the issue. I cannot control other people's negative emotions. Racism is still prevalent in our country, and I cannot control how others feel. So I try to ignore how they feel and concentrate on how I treat others. These are divisive times, and I may have concerns about elected officials. Instead of worrying about them, I can take steps to change things. I can become involved in local politics making sure people are registered to vote, and I can vote.

The primary point is not to let the things that concern us become worries that become anchors. Instead we must always seek ways to address our concerns or simply to discard them.

It is also important to understand that people can be our anchors. Many relationships fail because one or both partners feel that their relationship has stagnated. I have been married three times, so I know a little about failed relationships. When I moved to North Carolina from New York, I moved with my first wife and our two young sons, one a toddler and the other just a baby. I moved to become a disc jockey, and I loved my job. My problem was that at $90 a week I couldn't pay the bills and feed my family. Someone advised me to look into going to college and get money from the GI Bill. I enrolled at Wilkes Community College in Wilkesboro, NC, solely to get the extra money from the Veterans Administration. That extra money helped us make ends meet.

> Worrying about things we cannot control anchors us.

But going to college did something else. The young man who hated high school and who was told he was not college material fell in love with learning. A new world of history, of science, and of literature opened up for me, and I couldn't get enough. Literature, especially, impacted me. I didn't care whether I was reading poetry, short stories, essays, novels, and I didn't care whether the literature was American or British. It didn't matter. I loved it all. And I couldn't wait to share it with my wife. I began to dream of perhaps getting an Associate in Arts degree, and I began to dream of doing more with my life. But my wife did not share my enthusiasm. She was busy taking care of the boys and was not interested in what I was learning and in the things I wanted to discuss.

In a short period of time I began to feel restless, and I found that I was not always looking forward to going home. I loved the boys, but the relationship with my wife was becoming strained. At that time, I could not articulate what was happening, but looking back I realize I was beginning to feel weighed down. I wanted my life to move forward, but I couldn't see how that could happen. I had always envisioned moving forward as a family, but it was not happening.

I had always been faithful to my wife, but I began to spend as much time as I could at the college talking to my English teacher. She was a brilliant woman who was interested in the same things I was. Although she had a master's degree, and I was working on an AA degree, we were the same age, and we had many shared interests. It didn't take me long to fall for her. She pointed out a few years later that what I fell for was her mind.

At home I felt the anchor around my neck. At school, I felt free and could dream of possibilities. Less than two years after we moved to North Carolina, my wife left with our sons and moved to California where her parents lived. My unhappiness caused her to be unhappy, and the relationship unraveled. I was now free to explore other possibilities for my life. The English teacher and I married and had a son, but that marriage lasted only a couple of years. She was no anchor. In fact she encouraged me to finish my education, which I did.

In Chapter 3, I shared the rubber band analogy about forming bonds strong enough to withstand difficulties in relationships. Our bond never got as strong as it needed to be, and when difficulties arose, the bond broke. As I mentioned, she was not an anchor. If anything, I may have been an anchor to her. Once we divorced she went on to finish her education getting a doctorate and eventually becoming president of a community college.

Then I met Angela, and we formed a bond the moment we met. We gave to one another and reinforced the bond, one strong enough to withstand any issue. The bond has only grown stronger over time. Neither of us is an anchor to the other and have encouraged one another to grow, and that has boosted us over many hurdles.

Spouses can be anchors and so can other family members or friends. A question we should ask ourselves as we attempt to get over the hurdles in the way of our goals is, "Is someone or something holding me back? Do I have an anchor?" Identifying that anchor is an important step in clearing the hurdle. The next step is answering the question, "What am I going to do about it?" I would never recommend severing a relationship, especially a marriage that includes children. My first mother-in-law wrote me the sweetest letter asking me to stay with my first wife for the sake of the kids. But I couldn't. I was criticized (after both failed marriages) for being selfish, and I was. But as I mentioned in a previous chapter, "selfish" means taking care of the self before one can take care of others. And I was at a point (in both marriages) where I was no longer able to take care of myself and, thus, not be able to take care of and give to my wife and children.

Of course our own self-images can become anchors. I've mentioned self-confidence a number of times and will probably do so throughout this booklet. Self-confidence is essential to overcoming hurdles in life, and the lack of self-confidence is an anchor that not only prevents us from moving forward, but it is also something that weighs us down to the point we are unable to get over the hurdles to our happiness.

Shedding the anchor is rarely easy, but it is necessary if we know there are things or people in our lives that are holding us back and preventing us from reaching our goals.

Chapter 7: The Self-Inflicted Wound

I love movies and often find interesting scenes or dialogue that I can use to illustrate points I like to make. One such movie is *Excalibur*. It is the story of how the young squire, Arthur, pulled a sword from a stone and became king of England. People familiar with the legend of King Arthur know that in some versions, his most prized knight, Sir Lancelot, has an undying love for the queen, Guinevere.

In the movie, Lancelot feels a great deal of guilt for loving his king's wife. He worships his king and is loyal to him, yet he loves the king's wife. The guilt causes him to have a dream in which he finds himself wrestling with another knight. During the fight, Lancelot stabs the other knight. When he removes the helmet of the wounded knight, Lancelot sees himself. The shock of seeing himself causes Lancelot to waken with a cry of pain. The cry of pain is twofold. First, he notices that during the dream he actually stabbed himself, and he is gravely wounded. The second cry of pain is because he believes he betrayed his king.

Arthur gets his physicians to heal Lancelot who realizes he must leave the kingdom. He cannot bear to be near the woman he loves and the king he serves. Years later, Arthur is in a fierce battle with his son, Mordred, and the battle is not going well. He longs for his best knight, and seemingly out of nowhere, an older, unkempt, wild-eyed Lancelot appears. Lancelot's ferocity and skill enable him to subdue most of Mordred's men helping Arthur win the battle.

After the fight, Arthur finds Lancelot lying among the dead and wounded and knows his most favorite knight is dying. Arthur forgave Lancelot many years earlier and cradles his most loyal knight in his arms. Lancelot looks at Arthur and says, "It is the old wound, my King." And in Arthur's arms Lancelot dies.

The "old wound" was when Lancelot stabbed himself in his sleep. It was a self-inflicted wound. He wrestled with himself and stabbed himself because of the guilt he felt. The "old wound" stayed with him all of his life, and he finally succumbed to it.

I love the movie for its action, its story of courage and valor, its story of love and betrayal, its story of forgiveness, for the symbolism throughout, and for the lessons we can learn.

The "old wound" symbolizes Lancelot's guilt, and he never reconciled that guilt. Thus, *guilt is a self-inflicted wound.* And guilt, if not dealt with, becomes a difficult hurdle to overcome.

What are some "causes" of guilt? In other words, what makes people feel guilty? One cause is infidelity. Some people can go through life cheating on their spouses and not feeling the least bit guilty. It doesn't bother them that they have been unfaithful. For others, however, the guilt can become unbearable. That guilt is a hurdle that must be overcome if one is to move forward with his or her life.

Since infidelity is self-inflicted, the guilty person has no one to blame but himself. So he (or she) has to make a decision on how best to overcome the guilty feelings. One way is to admit to one's partner what happened. That could have both positive and negative consequences. A positive consequence is when the person who strayed feels unburdened once he has confessed his transgression. However, a negative consequence could be how the offended party takes to the news of infidelity.

When a person unburdens himself of the guilty feelings admitting to infidelity, that burden often ends up on the offended person. Now that person carries the knowledge of the affair, and images and thoughts could stay with that person for a long time. The longer it stays, the more likely it is that the relationship would begin to suffer. Doubt, mistrust, and other emotions could begin to seep into the relationship causing that relationship to suffer adding a hurdle that gets in the way of a successful partnership.

So the person who has cheated is faced with a dilemma. Keep the news of the transgression to himself and risk being burdened by guilt, or confess and ask for forgiveness and risk damaging the relationship.

In order to make the best choice, people need to go back to the rubber band analogy in Chapter 3. I already referred to that analogy in the previous chapter, and I may refer to it a few more times because it reinforces the importance of establishing a strong relationship. If the bond is strong, very strong, the relationship should be able to withstand the openness and honesty of a confession. If that bond is not strong, a confession could cause the relationship to end. In a case where the guilty person is not sure whether the relationship could withstand the news of infidelity, it would be better not to unburden one's self. Unburdening the guilt is a temporary solution but could lead to a longtime problem. A fair question to ask oneself is, "Is my relationship strong enough to withstand the truth?"

There are other causes of feeling guilty, but most of them stem from choices we make. And if guilt is a self-inflicted wound, then the depth of our guilt is often proportional to the depth of the wound. Lancelot's wound was deep caused by impaling himself on his sword. Infidelity is a deep wound. But some wounds are not so deep, and people could deal with guilt in those situations.

Once when I was coaching, a vote was taken for Coach-of-the-Year. I had had a really good season, and my players won a few awards. I wanted to win an award also. So I voted for myself for coach-of-the-year. There were no regulations prohibiting a coach to vote for him or herself, but common courtesy was such that voting for one's self was just not done. I was named Coach-of-the-Year by a 7-1 vote. There were eight of us who voted, so no one knew I had voted for myself. But I knew, and I felt bad. I would have felt much better voting for someone else and winning by a 6-2 vote.

> Guilt, if not dealt with, becomes a difficult hurdle to overcome.

The guilt I felt was not deep, and I got over it quickly. The incident comes to my mind from time to time, as it did when I was writing this chapter, and the remembering is a reminder of an action I should not have taken, but I am not burdened by guilt over that incident. It was not a deep wound, but many decisions do cause deep wounds.

The deepest wounds I caused were my divorces. In both cases –without getting real specific – something happened, and we began to grow apart. But I was the one who initiated the divorce in both cases. I know I hurt my ex-wives and my children. I did feel guilty, but I understood then, as I do now, that the guilt was my own doing. Others tried to make me feel guilty by their actions and words toward me. One former friend actually turned his back on me when I saw him a few weeks after I had moved out. But I realized that nothing he nor anyone else could do could actually make me feel guilty. I made the right decisions for myself, but that did not lessen my guilt. But I knew that if I was going to be happy and have a chance at a decent life, I had to make those decisions. I would never suggest that people who are unhappy should seek a divorce. I would suggest that they first seek to understand the causes of the difficulties and see if they could resolve their differences.

But my strongest advice is that people should never contemplate marriage before discussing and resolving all issues/concerns prior to tying the knot. Developing the strong bond before getting married helps when difficulties begin.

Generally, the deepest wounds causing the deepest guilt are when we hurt other people. It is in these cases when people need to decide how best to rid themselves of their guilt. In Chapter 3, I mentioned what Jesus said in Matthew 18:15 about how to deal with someone who has offended you. We are expected to make the first move, but if we have hurt someone and feel guilty about it, it is often very difficult to make that first move.

Making the first move could open ourselves to being hurt if the person will not forgive us. But making that first move is a step in removing our own guilt. And that guilt must be removed if we are to overcome that hurdle to success and happiness. We cannot be wracked with guilt and be happy at the same time.

So, step 1 in overcoming guilt that often keeps us from moving forward is our understanding that guilt is our own doing. It is a *self-inflicted wound.* Not being able to accept that premise causes people with guilty feelings to blame others for that guilt. Not taking responsibility for one's actions creates a hurdle that is difficult to overcome.

The next step, obviously, once we own that our guilty feelings are of our own making, is to address the cause of the guilty feeling. Then we take action and move on. Sounds simple, and it really could be. My guilty feelings about leaving my respective marriages were caused by my own actions. Other people's negative reactions toward me hurt somewhat, but I couldn't blame them for how I felt. I accepted the responsibility for my actions and, over time, reached out to both ex-wives in an attempt to make amends. I was one for two! But once I reached out, regardless of the responses I received, I knew I had to move on. Wallowing in self-pity and allowing guilt to keep one from moving forward can be an almost insurmountable hurdle.

So, we must accept that the guilty feelings we experience are of our own making. Then we address the cause(s) of the guilty feelings, and move on. If we cannot move on, we find ourselves stymied by our own actions and inactions, blocked by a hurdle we cannot overcome.

Chapter 8: The Plow Horse and the Thoroughbred

One of the things I used to do when I taught was to walk around the room as I talked. I could never lecture from the front of the class. I paced. I walked around. One advantage of walking around a lot was that I could always position myself near a student or two who might have been on the verge of "acting out." I rarely had to say anything to the student who needed my attention. I just had to be close enough to give him pause before he did something that would have gotten him in trouble.

But all the walking around caught the attention of one of my students one day. He said, "Coach Vandett. Why do you strut so much?" I replied, "I don't strut." Almost in unison, the rest of the class said, "Yes, you do!"

I thought for a moment, looked at the class and said, "Have you ever seen a plow horse working in a field, plodding along with its head hanging down?" The students nodded. Then I asked, "Have you ever seen a thoroughbred race horse as it is walking toward the starting gate with its chest out, shoulders back, and its head held high?" Again they nodded. I said, "Well, y'all. I ain't no plow horse."

Since that time I have tried to live my life as a thoroughbred instead of as a plow horse. That simply means holding my head high no matter the circumstances. Like most people in this world, I have been knocked down a number of times. I've been hurt and at times felt there was no way for me to overcome the problems I had. But the image of the thoroughbred would come into my mind, and I believed I could overcome my issues by first believing in myself.

In Chapter 2, "The Pit and the Ladder," I mentioned that the first step out of the pit of depression is to concentrate on the bottom rung of the ladder as one works his or her way out of the pit. For me, that first step would be simply believing in myself. And believing in myself is to allow myself to be proud of who I am regardless of my circumstances. Proverbs 16:18 states, "Pride goeth before a fall." However, that does not mean that one cannot be proud of himself or herself. Being proud of oneself means that a person believes in himself and believes he has the strength to overcome the hurdles in his life.

I have seen individuals in a group who often fold into themselves. By that I mean that their self-image is such that they are not necessarily proud of who they are, that they lack self-confidence, and you can see them with their heads down and their shoulders folding inward. It's almost as though they are trying to hide in plain sight. Of course they would never refer to themselves as plow horses, but, metaphorically, that's what they are.

Self-confidence is such an important trait in overcoming hurdles. The key word is "self." Self-confidence comes from the "self." No one can give another person self-confidence. And that is a hurdle because if one lacks self-confidence and realizes no one else can give him self-confidence, he may be at a loss as to how to strengthen his self-image. One cannot enhance his or her self-image by simply "folding" into him/her self. An important step is not to isolate one's self.

When I graduated from high school I was not filled with a great deal of self-confidence. I went in the military at age 17 and soon found that I was capable of doing things well. I was often asked by the DI (drill instructor) to do extra things (paperwork, forging signatures – seriously – and a number of other things), and I began to feel a little self-respect. I didn't realize at the time that it was my actions that were enhancing the way I saw myself.

In tech school, I was given leadership positions, and after arriving at Fort Benning, I was given more. I moved up in rank in minimum time, and we began training in the field (to prepare for Viet Nam, but I did not know this at the time), and I was awarded command responsibilities. Soon after arriving in Viet Nam, I found myself in leadership positions. Two months into working in the First Air Cavalry, I was given charge of two- or three man teams going on operations. I held those responsibilities when transferred to the First Infantry Division. I gained a great deal of self-confidence from my four years in the military and my experience in Viet Nam.

Following my discharge, my friend Tracy, whom I met in Vietnam, and I moved to the Los Angeles area where I lived for four years. I started going to school – Los Angeles Valley College – and was doing well. But I had gotten married, my wife lost her job, and I had to quit school and go to work. My self confidence became stronger once I began to work at a finance company. There was a two-year program assistant managers had to go through before being considered for their own offices. It took me less time than that. Within a year I was a branch manager and doing very well. I worked long hours and made good money, but I was unhappy. I wanted something else, and that something else was to be a disc jockey. So, I enrolled in a broadcasting school at night in Hollywood, and took a three month course. I quit the finance company and took a job with the post office while I continued going to school at night. Following graduation I sent audition tapes throughout the country but never received any positive responses.

A month after graduation, a major earthquake hit (February, 1971) in the San Fernando Valley that shook us up (literally and figuratively), and a month later I packed up the family (wife, one son, and one on the way) and moved back to New York. I had to work three jobs to make ends meet in New York. I waxed floors with my stepfather from 4:00 – 5:30 a.m., worked for the post office from 6:00 a.m. – 3:00 p.m. sorting and delivering mail, then worked as a night manager in a recreational center from 6:00 -11:00 p.m. I thought that was destined to be my life – obviously not enhancing my self-image - until I received a call in September 1971 from a radio station in Wilkesboro, NC, offering me a job. I took it.

> No one can give another person self-confidence.

There is a saying about being a big fish in a small pond, and that is what I became. I found out that I was good at what I did and received promotions fairly quickly. Soon I became the program director and the sports director, and, as in the TV show "Cheers," everyone knew my name. That little bit of notoriety helped me "strut around like a thoroughbred!"

I wasn't able to feed a family of four on a disc jockey's salary, so I enrolled in a local community college simply to get extra funds from the G. I Bill. But my age (26) and my self-confidence helped me do very well in school, and following graduation from the community college, I went to Appalachian State University for two years and received a degree in English while still working full time at the radio station.

My self-confidence propelled me in one direction, but that direction took me away from my wife. We separated, and she and the boys moved back to California to be with her parents. Following graduation from ASU, I was able to get a job as a teacher and a coach. I was successful in both areas, and many honors came my way. As I looked back at my career, I realized that I was good at most everything I did, and that helped my self-image. The one thing at which I was not good was marriage. Within a few years of working as a teacher and a coach, I married and divorced again. Two failed marriages did not help how I saw myself, but I knew there was something in me that could help me push myself, help me not to settle, and help me walk with my head held high. I also began to realize how important it was to be around positive people.

We are a community-oriented species. We don't do loneliness well. We are not hermits by nature. But it is important to surround ourselves with people who can uplift us, not drag us down. Most of us strive for some type of equality among the people with whom we interact. There are some people who feel others are above them, and they want to be equal to them. But instead of working to lift themselves up, they try to bring the others down to their level thus achieving, in their minds, equality. Obviously, these people need to be avoided. They do not help others over hurdles; they put hurdles in the way.

A key barometer in choosing with which kind of people to associate is simply, "Do I like to be around this person?" Some people gravitate toward others because of a need to belong, to feel part of a group. In and of itself, that is not necessarily bad. There is nothing wrong with being part of a group. But we should always ask ourselves how we feel about the people in the group. Do we belong because it's cool to be in a group, or do we belong because we enjoy the interactions with the group members? Do we feel confident among the people with whom we interact, or do we feel intimidated by them? Of course, if it's a group associated with negativity (white supremacists, gangs, etc.), it's best to find another that could enhance your self-image.

I married a third time to a wonderful woman who lifts me up and with whom I enjoy being. I learned from the mistakes I made in my previous marriages and have benefitted from that relationship. My wife, Angela, helps me walk with my head held high.

§

I love the "Serenity Prayer." *God, grant me the Serenity to accept the things I cannot change, the Courage to change the things I can, and the Wisdom to know the difference.*

Knowing the difference is important. The difference between people who lift you up or who tear you down. The difference between activities that build one's self-esteem or activities designed to cause pain and heartache. The difference between the things about which one is capable of doing and the things that will add hurdles to one's life. The things that would enable one to walk as a thoroughbred or walk as a plow horse. Knowing these differences and acting accordingly will always enhance our self-esteem and help us over the hurdles.

Chapter 9: YAHOO/ "What, Me Worry?"

I remember as a youngster loving to read MAD magazine. There was so much information and wisdom in that publication. The main character was Alfred E. Neuman whose face was on the cover of the magazine. His motto was "What, me worry?" I liked that slogan, but I was too young to realize that worrying solved no problems. In Chapter 6, I shared the story of a girl's father who asked me, "How many problems have you ever solved by worrying about them?" When I was 19, that statement made sense and has since had a profound impact on how I approach life and its hurdles. But when I was 10, "What, me worry?" was just an interesting saying. It didn't cause me not to worry about things. In fact, at that age I worried a great deal.

We were living in New York at that time, and my mother was married to my first stepfather who was a mean, vile, drunken SOB. He often beat me for – in my opinion – no reason, and I was deathly afraid of him. When I was seven years old I saw him cut my mother's neck with a kitchen paring knife. I worried about her and about me. I didn't know how to face my fears.

One day he "lost it," took a shotgun and shot up the house. My mother escaped to a neighbor's house with my baby sister and called the police. My brother and other sister – my stepfather's children – and I were in school at the time. My mother and her brother, a policeman, came to the school and took us to his house. Three days later we were in Youngstown, Ohio, and a year after that we were living in a housing project. For many years, when I met someone who was obviously drunk, I began to tremble and worry.

Worrying was a natural thing to do for a young person who had yet to develop a strong inner self. As a teenager in the projects, I learned to handle myself and began to have a better self-image. I had a reputation as a good fighter, and not too many people wanted to mess with me. That was good because I didn't know how good a fighter I really was. I just had that reputation, a reputation basically built on one punch.

We had just moved to the projects. I was 12 years old and hanging around with a bunch of guys. One afternoon we were playing football in a big field, and I noticed my tennis shoe was untied. I bent down to tie it, and as I began to get up, the leader of the group (we were not officially a "gang") pushed me down. As I began to get up a second time, he did it again. He was the leader of the group because everyone was afraid of him. He was a bully. But I had had enough. As I started to rise for the third time he stepped toward me again. This time I came up too fast for him to get to me, and I threw a punch that started from near my shoe and ended up squarely on his jaw. He went down. That one punch was really enough, but I jumped on him and hit him a few more times before the other guys pulled me off of him. He stammered something about his just messing with me, and I let it go at that. But he never bullied us again, and my reputation was built. My inner self was becoming stronger, and I was worrying about things less and less.

Years after I accepted "never worrying about things over which I have no control," (Chapter 6) I heard about the YAHOO philosophy of dealing with issues instead of worrying about them. It is now something in which I believe strongly, and I share it with folks as often as I can.

YAHOO – Y, A, H, O, O – stands for –You Always Have Other Options. I often give motivational speeches, and I try to incorporate the YAHOO philosophy whenever I can. I try to get people to see that we all have other options if something is not working out as we planned. This belief is especially useful when facing hurdles that are difficult to overcome.

Christians often say that when God closes a door He often opens a window. In essence, God is giving us other options if we fail or lose out on certain things. The key is to believe there really are other options. Not believing in other options creates an almost insurmountable hurdle because one feels there is nowhere else to turn. That feeling leads to depression which leads to a sense of hopelessness. It is essential to believe there are other options, to work hard to determine what they may be, and to take the best option(s) available.

While YAHOO is a convenient acronym for stating folks will always have other options, simply accepting that premise means nothing if we do not actively seek those other options. The first step is to truly believe there are other options when our first attempt has failed. The next step is to actively seek what those options could be. If we do not look for other options, we allow our first failed attempt to be a hurdle that would be difficult to overcome.

A simple example is someone having a goal of getting a college education. The first step could be applying to a college. Often, though, such applications could be denied. The door to a college education is closed. Now what should the person do? There have been many people who, when their initial applications to a college were not approved, simply quit trying, found decent paying jobs, and continued on with their lives never realizing the goal of a college education.

As I mentioned in Chapter 2, "The Pit and the Ladder," the ladder becomes an option for people who feel as though they are in the pit of depression. Identifying the steps of the ladder is essential, but it's also important to realize that if a step seems difficult to attain, consider YAHOO. Look for what other options there may be. In the above example of applying to go to a college, if the first step (applying to a specific college) is not attainable because the application has been denied, a second step could be an alternative path. Many states have junior colleges or community colleges, and these schools virtually accept everyone. I took that path as many others have done and continue to do. I couldn't get into a four-year school when I first moved to North Carolina because I had never taken the Scholastic Aptitude Test (SAT). So I went to a community college, took college transfer courses, and transferred to a university that accepted the Associate in Arts degree in lieu of the SAT.

> # YAHOO
>
> You Always Have Other Options.

A more serious issue facing people who feel they have no options is being alone due to the loss of a loved one or by breaking up with someone who had been a focal part of their lives. I've known a number of people who were devastated when someone left them. Most of those people felt there was nothing left in their lives. They didn't know what to do. That's when we should help others see the three step YAHOO process:

1. *Believe there are other options*
2. *Explore what options there are*
3. *Choose the best one(s) and act*

There are other serious goals people have difficulty in achieving (e.g. overcoming addictions, infidelities, financial problems, etc.), and YAHOO can come into play with any of these concerns. Again, the first step is believing there are other options; step two is actively seeking what those options could be; and step three is choosing the best option. In most cases, trying to solve problems alone can be disheartening. People give up when their first attempt to solve a problem on their own fails instead of looking to others for support.

No philosophy or program is foolproof. Twelve-step programs work for some but not for others. But if one thing doesn't work, something else just might. The key is to never, ever give up. There are other options, and we must always actively seek them.

Chapter 10: Lessons from

"The Wizard of Oz"

I mentioned in Chapter 7, "The Self-Inflicted Wound," that I often find inspirational things from movies. One such movie is *The Wizard of Oz*. I remember when I first saw that movie. I was about seven or eight years old, and my older cousin Joan took us to a movie. I had never heard of the movie and of course did not know it had been released many years before. So I didn't know what to expect.

The movie started in black and white, which I was accustomed to seeing (we had a black and white television at home). When Dorothy's house landed in the Land of Oz, the movie suddenly turned to color. I was awed, amazed, stunned, thrilled beyond belief. I remember my first trip to Ebbets Field in Brooklyn to see the Dodgers play and how amazed I was to see how green a real ballfield was. That was a thrilling moment. I experienced that same amazed, thrilling feeling in the movie.

We all know the main characters and what they hoped to get from the great wizard. The Scarecrow wanted a brain. The Tin Man wanted a heart. The Cowardly Lion wanted courage. And Dorothy simply wanted to go home.

Along the way, the Scarecrow figured out how to save Dorothy. That took brains. The Tin Man cried when he thought Dorothy would never come back from being taken – in fact he cried when he stepped on a bug (in the book). A person can't cry if he doesn't have a heart. And the Cowardly Lion was ready to fight the flying monkeys (I had nightmares for days after seeing them for the first time). One doesn't take on the witch's army without having a great deal of courage.

At the end of the movie, Glinda, the good witch, tells Dorothy that all she has to do to go home is click her heels three times and say "There's no place like home."

The lesson learned is that all of the characters – Dorothy, the Scarecrow, the Tin Man, and the Cowardly Lion – had what they wanted and needed inside of them all along. And so do we.

The most difficult thing for many people to realize is that within each of us is the ability to achieve our goals. We have brains, compassion, and courage but often lack the wherewithal to draw upon those traits – primarily because we don't realize or don't believe those traits are within us.

Our biggest failing is that often we do not believe we are smart enough to figure out how to overcome the obstacles in our lives. Of course, there are those with low-emotional intelligence who do not possess the mental acuity needed to overcome issues, but they are a very small percentage of the world's population. The rest of us do have that ability. So why don't we rely on our own intelligence?

One reason is the dependence on social media. It is the prime reason I no longer post or read posts on Facebook (and I do not have a Twitter account!). Too many people formulate their opinions based on what they read on social media or what their political party tells them they should believe. The political Left does not want to turn America into a socialist country, as those on the right believe, and the political Right does not want to turn America into a whites-only country a la' Nazi Germany, as those on the left believe. Yet people believe what they read and see on social media. These people are not using their brains to overcome personal hurdles. They are not using their brains or relying on common sense. Instead, they are creating obstacles to peace and happiness for themselves and others by their dependence on social media instead of their own brains to tell them what to believe. I plan to build a monument to the first person I meet whose mind was changed by a Facebook post.

> Within each of us is the ability to achieve our goals.

While the capacity for compassion – heart – is within us, many people do not exhibit a compassionate nature. Compassion simply is the ability to sympathize and empathize with others as well as to feel a genuine concern about the welfare of other people. For some, it is easier to hate than to make an effort to understand people different from themselves. Many people call themselves Christians and firmly believe in God, yet they treat others and make comments about certain groups of people that would truly make Jesus weep. Having a stone cold heart is a hurdle keeping many people from enjoying the kind of life God wants for us all.

Many of us can relate to the Cowardly Lion when it comes to courage. For me, the Serenity Prayer helps me focus on the word "courage."

God, grant me the Serenity to accept the things I cannot change, the Courage to change the things I can, and the Wisdom to know the difference.

Courage is having the inner strength to take action in a given situation. Many people, just like the the Cowardly Lion, do not believe they have the courage to take action when that action is needed. They have the "plow horse" mentality, schlumping through life with their heads held down never believing they could make a difference, never believing they have what it takes to be successful, to reach a goal. It takes someone with the "thoroughbred" mentality to realize he or she has the courage to face any challenge.

My wife and I have that courage. We needed it when we hit bottom financially, and we needed it when we lost our son. We knew we HAD to have the strength and courage to overcome those obstacles. We knew we would not, could not give up. And we not only turned to outside resources (home sale, friends, church, etc.) but also to our inner strengths. We knew we had within us what we needed to overcome our hurdles, and we relied upon our inner strengths.

A prevailing theme throughout this little book is a belief in the inner self. That we have within us all we need to overcome obstacles, to reach our goals, to be happy. Without that belief, overcoming hurdles is a daunting task.

Chapter 11: The Tree of Life

I once asked my Sunday school class why God kicked Adam and Eve out of the Garden of Eden. The predominant answer was because they disobeyed Him by eating the fruit of the tree. Genesis 3:22-23 has these words: *"Then the LORD God said, 'See the man has become like one of us, knowing good from evil; and now, he might reach out his hand and take also from the tree of life, and eat, and live forever'."*

Adam and Eve had eaten from the Tree of Knowledge thus knowing good from evil. God did not want them also to eat from the Tree of Life and thus live forever.

God doesn't want us to live forever, but He does want us to have a rich, full life. The founding fathers of our country used the phrase "the pursuit of happiness" in stating what should be a fundamental right of all people. The Tree of Life offers some insight in steps to achieving happiness and personal fulfillment.

I googled "Tree of Life," and found many interesting articles. One listed some features of trees: ground, seed, roots, trunk, branches, leaves, and fruit. It all starts with good ground and good seed. Good seed on barren ground and bad seed on good ground will not produce any fruit. We are the seed. Whether we are good or bad depends solely on how we choose to live our lives. If the environment in which we find ourselves is a strong one (good ground), our negative, even destructive choices will not produce the fruit (goals) for which we hope. Conversely if we try to make good decisions but surround ourselves in negative environments, we will not achieve our goals.

The pursuit of happiness is enhanced when we strive to make good decisions and put ourselves in positive situations. When we can do that, we develop stability (strong roots), grow stronger as individuals (trunk), develop relationships (branches), find blessings from those relationships (leaves), and begin to realize some of our goals (fruit).

The Tree of Life symbolizes many different things for people of varying beliefs, but it is generally seen as symbolizing strength and unity. As I mentioned in the introduction, this is not a scholarly treatise. So I won't comment on the various things the Tree symbolizes. Suffice to say that not only can we use the Tree of Life as a metaphor of bettering ourselves, but we can also learn from the Tree itself. For me, looking at and reading about the Tree helps me to realize I have great potential – "Mighty oaks from little acorns grow." Believing the tiny acorn will grow into a mighty oak reinforces my faith. I, too, can be more than a tiny acorn. I look at the tree and realize the tree has a purpose. And so do I. Potential and Purpose.

Potential is another trait we have within us (similar to brains, heart, and courage). But potential for most of us is rarely tapped fully. And if we do not believe we have the potential to grow, be happy, and make a positive difference in the lives of others, we create a hurdle that stymies our growth.

Realizing our potential becomes difficult when we are unsure of our goals, our aims in life – our purpose. If you don't know where you're going, how will you know how to get there? Or whether you have arrived? Happiness is an elusive, vague term. Most of us say we want to be happy, but we are not quite sure what happiness truly is and, thus, cannot develop a path towards achieving that goal. I'll discuss more about "purpose" in Chapter 13.

It is essential for us to examine our lives and to answer the question, "What will make me happy; what will make me content with the person I am?" The 100 meter dash vs. the 100 meter hurdle race only makes sense when we can identify what the finish line represents.

Once we can identify the thing or things that will make us happy, that will help us be successful in life, we then tap into our potential to take the necessary steps toward reaching our goals.

> "Mighty oaks from little acorns grow."

Someone once told me I had the potential to be an excellent salesman. He said I had a great personality, people liked me, I was a hard worker, I was a dedicated person, and I was intelligent. But what I didn't tell him was that I didn't have the nerve, the courage to be a salesman. I did have the nerve and the courage to do other things, but not to be a salesman. I didn't have the strength it would have taken to work at a job solely on commission. My financial situation at the time was not one in which I felt comfortable not having a guaranteed income. I knew being a salesman would not make me happy, so it made no sense to me to use whatever potential I had pursuing something I didn't really want to do.

Potential only matters when it is used to pursue the goals that are truly important. Once I decided I wanted to further my education, I pursued that goal vigorously.

I have had a number of goals, each that had hurdles that I had to clear to reach the goals, but they all fell under the subjective goal of simply being happy.

I realized that one step toward being satisfied with my life was to further my education. I wanted a master's degree, and I wanted to get a doctoral degree. So attaining each degree became a separate goal with a separate path with its own set of hurdles. I used the potential that my friend said would make me a good salesman to work on the goals of getting the extra degrees. Not so sure that my personality was a factor, but I was a hard worker, I was dedicated, and I was intelligent (still am).

While there were many hurdles to my getting the degrees I wanted, I had the inner strength (potential) as well as the belief in myself to overcome those hurdles. Rather than allow the hurdles – distance to school, time constraints posed by current job situations, money, family, etc. – to keep me from attempting to reach my goals, I relied on the qualities that were within me to face and overcome each hurdle.

For me, the Tree of Life is an image I can use to remind me that I have the right to pursue the life that God has made available for all of us. We each have different sets of obstacles. Socioeconomic status, racism, elitism, inferiority complexes, hatred, and many other things can be and are obstacles for many people. But we all have a God-given right to be happy, and we all should use the potential we have to pursue that dream.

I remember telling a class one day not to let others tell them that their high school years and their college years were the best years of their lives. I pointed out that if one graduates from high school at 18 years old and/or college at 22 years old, and if those were the best years of their lives, what could they possibly have to look forward to for the next 70 or 80 years?

We should look forward to every year of our lives and strive to make each year the best it could possibly be.

Chapter 12: We Never Get Out of Middle School

I can remember a psychology class I took in college where I learned that much of our personality is formed by the time we are twelve years old. Middle school age. The hope is that we grow and strengthen the good qualities and learn how to avoid the negative qualities we had when we were twelve.

A problem, however, for many people is that they never grow beyond what they were when they were twelve years old. The need to belong to a group is strong among middle school students. Young people who had many friends in elementary school begin selecting and sorting when they get to middle school. We all know someone (maybe ourselves?) who had good "friends" turn their backs on them for some perceived slight. These friends excluded us from their group, and we had to find another group.

Sadly, that type of behavior often never goes away. People in their sixties and seventies splinter off of a larger group and ignore people with whom they once interacted.

I've often heard that there are two things about which friends and family should never argue: politics and religion. I mentioned in an earlier chapter about the negative aspects of social media, and never is that negativity more evident than in people's reactions to comments on social media concerning politics and religion.

Social media is not a forum for discussion. It is a platform for shouting out one's views while denigrating opposing viewpoints. And it is this type of behavior that causes rifts among families and friends. The highly charged political atmosphere offers no room for middle-of-the-road viewpoints. Centrist views are seen as weak views, and people who look for ways to compromise and bring people together for the common good are seen as weak individuals who are afraid to take a side.

And taking a side rather than working together brings us back to middle school. Groups in middle school were constantly being reformed through inclusions and exclusions based on which "side" someone took. I understand that type of behavior among middle school students. I do not understand that same behavior among adults.

We all want to belong. And when we are excluded from groups of people we thought were friends, or when family members turn away from us because of how we may view the political landscape or how we perceive religion, hurdles appear that can block our path to success and happiness.

A very important thing to consider is how we react when we realize people whom we thought were friends no longer include us in the things they do. Our first reaction is usually to wonder why we are being excluded, then, often, to feel rejected and become depressed. It's human nature to feel we have done something to offend someone. And in some cases we probably have, but often what others see as transgressions are not things we see as being negative.

For example, let's say when you were in middle school you begin being nice to someone other kids rejected. That act might make the group to which you belonged look at you differently and wonder whether you had the same "values" as they did. So they begin to pull away from you and begin to exclude you. They see your friendliness toward a person whom they perceive to be beneath them as a transgression. You see that behavior as a natural act of kindness toward another person.

Often, especially in middle and high school, how people dress, what they say, how they behave often causes them to be excluded. And that exclusion often causes young people to become depressed and isolated. Being excluded from a group at middle and high school age can be painful.

> The closing of minds in discussing either religion or politics can be an almost insurmountable hurdle.

That pain can also be experienced by adults, who are often excluded from groups. I put the word "values" in quotation marks in a preceding paragraph because values come into play a great deal when groups are formed and reformed. Especially religious groups.

I was christened as a Catholic and even attended two different Catholic schools while growing up. As a youth I embraced the Catholic religion and even served as an altar boy. I got away from religion as I got older but came back to church after Angela and I married. She had grown up as a Methodist, so I began attending the Methodist church.

Once we began going to church together, we joined a Sunday school class, and we became very close to the members of that class. I grew in my faith journey, and we enjoyed the fellowship and friendship of a number of folks in that group.

We moved to Hickory, NC, in 2003 and joined a Methodist church in that community. Our positive experience with the Sunday school class in North Wilkesboro, where we had lived for 24 years, caused us to look for just the right Sunday school class in our new church.

We found a class that we loved and are still members of that class. I mentioned earlier about not discussing religion and politics if you want to keep your friends as well as keep your family together. Well, it's hard not to discuss religion in a Sunday school class!

My wife and I are fairly liberal in our religious views. We believe in the inerrant Word of God (capital "W") in the Bible, but we also believe that the words (small "w") are open for interpretation. Once I began teaching our class, I realized that not everyone in the class looked at Scripture as I did. Many take the words in the Bible literally, and many others see scripture as open to interpretation. I learned early on to provide opportunities for people to share their thoughts without taking sides. Some people, especially those who take scripture literally (God created the world in six 24-hour days), get very passionate about their beliefs and close their minds to other viewpoints.

The same can be said for people's political views. Generally, I have found, people who are ultra conservative in their political views are very passionate about what they believe and usually close their minds to other political views. The same can be said for those on the far left who refuse to listen to things different from what they believe.

The closing of minds in discussing either religion or politics can be an almost insurmountable hurdle to maintain friendships or relationships, which, in turn, creates hurdles to peace, harmony, and happiness.

The close-mindedness of some people is akin to attitudes many of us had in middle school (when I was that age it was called junior high school). Not being willing to accept people different from ourselves – whether the differences are by race, ethnicity, socio-economic status, origins of birth, religion, politics, or sexual orientation – causes hurdles at any age.

The only solution is to "grow up!"

As a Christian, especially when I went to Catholic school and to mass, I saw many depictions of Jesus. And in virtually all of them he is holding his arms wide open, inviting all to join him. He is not depicted as standing stoically, arms folded across his chest, scowling at those who don't see things the way he does. "Growing up" means being as open as Jesus in looking at the world. Hurdles fall by the wayside when we expand our minds and at least consider ideas different from ours and people different from ourselves. We don't always have to agree with others, but we do not have to hate and exclude those different from us as often happens in middle school.

Hopefully, we can all find ways to grow up, be secure in who we are, and begin to knock down hurdles.

Chapter 13: Keeping the Main Thing the Main Thing

I love the title of this chapter. We've all heard that saying many times. *Keep the main thing the main thing.* Makes sense, sorta. Who would disagree with that statement? Heads nod, and people say, "You're right. We have to keep the main thing the main thing." But just what does that phrase mean?

To me, *the main thing* is that one strong purpose/ reason for living our lives and for doing what we should be doing with our lives. The word "keep" means, in this case, "focus." In other words we should maintain our focus on what is really important in our lives.

I had been a frequent user of social media, especially Facebook. When I first joined Facebook, I was excited about the "friends" with whom I began to connect. Friends from my youth, former students I taught, former players I coached, people with whom I worked, and family members all began to converse with me through Facebook. Initially it was a rush for me to connect with people from whom I had not heard in years. But over time, things began to change. A few years ago I ran for public office, and I made the mistake of reading Facebook posts about my candidacy. My true "friends" were complimentary and proud of me. But others who read my posts were vile in their comments. I have no problem with people disagreeing with me. I do have a problem with how some choose to disagree.

Politics have shown people's true colors when it comes to social media. There is absolutely no middle ground when it comes to how people view issues, policies, and politicians. They love their side and hate the other side, no matter how correct the other side may be. For some, it's "facts be damned. I believe what I believe. It's probably Fake News anyway."

People have become so narrow-minded that it causes them to lose focus on what is truly important in life. That narrow-mindedness is a huge hurdle that gets in the way of overcoming life's difficulties.

Of course a major hurdle is determining what is "truly important in life." Would what is most important in life be the same for everyone? Probably not. What is truly important could probably be put into four categories: 1) other people, 2) tangible things, 3) personal achievements, and 4) one's self.

Let's take a look at these four categories in reverse order. If one's self is the most important thing in life, then keeping the main thing the main thing would simply be about satisfying one's greed and trying to establish control over everything and everyone in a person's life. My first thought would be that that type of focus would not bring someone true happiness, but there are too many examples in this country of people who have lived their lives as though no one was nearly as important as they were. They spend their entire lives feeding their own egos and striving for success without regard for the feelings or lives of other people. In essence, they have kept the main thing – themselves – the main thing.

Personal achievement is a goal – and a worthy goal – of many people. Many people today are able to further their education through online programs while still maintaining their current occupations. Personal achievement is not just furthering one's education. It can be defined in a number of ways. For me, however, it *was* furthering my education.

As I mentioned earlier, I went to a community college simply to receive money from the G. I. Bill in order to pay my bills. But I fell in love with school, transferred to a university, graduated and began a career in education.

Early in my teaching career I flirted with the idea of getting a master's degree. The thought of a doctorate never crossed my mind. But I didn't pursue an advanced degree because I just didn't have the time.

Then, after fourteen years of teaching, some honors came my way, and I had a year out of the classroom during which I served as a Teacher Recruiter traveling around the state attending conferences and extolling the virtues of teaching to hundreds of high school students. The flexible schedule allowed me to pursue the master's degree.

I began a career in administration starting off as a middle school assistant principal. My goal at that time was to be a high school principal. Within two years I did become a principal, but it was at an elementary school. At that time, I still did not have obtaining a doctorate as a goal. Then a strange thing happened.

One Sunday morning before the worship service, many of us in the congregation were enjoying a cup of coffee in the fellowship hall. I was approached by a man I knew but with whom I had rarely spoken. He told me that forty years earlier, a man had offered to help him get into Columbia University in New York City. The man, John, was a retired school superintendent, and he knew I was a school administrator. Although we had barely exchanged a dozen words since Angela and I joined the church, he asked me if I would accept his offer to help me get into Columbia University so that I could pursue a doctorate. I really didn't know what to say, but I accepted his offer. His only stipulation was that I was to help someone else get into Columbia if I were to be accepted. Five months later, I was attending my first class on the campus of Columbia University on New York's Upper Westside.

I would be the first to say that I am not sure how God works His wonders. I believe in God wholeheartedly, but I do not know when and why He acts. Although I pray for my favorite teams to win games, I doubt He is a big football fan. Let me rephrase that. If there is a heaven, there is football in heaven, so God could be a fan, just not necessarily a fan of *my* favorite teams. But I am convinced that my faith somehow came in to play with my getting to be able to apply to Columbia and my being accepted. When I contacted the person John suggested, he told me there were three North Carolinians in the cohort that had started the previous year. He told me their names, and one of them, Ann, was someone who sang in the choir of the church that Angela attended growing up in the small town of Creedmoor, NC. I knew of this person, but we had never really met. I made an effort to talk to her the next time Angela and I went to Creedmoor. When we did go to Creedmoor a few weeks later, I met Ann after church and told her I was applying to Columbia University in the same program she was in. She got very excited and said she would call the director of the program the next day and give me a recommendation.

> A major hurdle is determining what is "truly important in life."

Neither John nor Ann really knew me all that well, yet – and here is where God comes in – one person in a church fellowship hall makes me an offer I cannot refuse, and another person in a church choir offers to give me a recommendation. The connections to church were not a coincidence, and I honestly felt as though God was leading me where He wanted me to go. Thus, my focus, my "main thing," my desire for personal growth, became a reality. Oh, and I did as John had asked by helping two of my friends to get into the program at Columbia.

For some people, the acquisition of tangible things is what is truly important to them, is their focus. I am technically not a Baby Boomer – too old by a year. But I have had some of the same weaknesses many boomers have had. Following World War II, many people began to enjoy a little prosperity. Jobs were plentiful, and many of them did not require even a high school education. With jobs came decent wages, and with money in hand many people looked to purchase as many "things" as they could. But there are too many examples of people being depressed and unhappy regardless of the amount of "things" they have for getting more things to be the main thing for everyone. Trying to make one's self look good by "keeping up with the Joneses" rarely brings about true happiness. Making one's self feel important by external acquisitions doesn't work for most people. However, that is not to say one should never try to feel important or to enhance one's sense of self-worth. It's just that accumulating "things" is rarely the answer.

Obviously, many "things" are important. I joined the military when I was seventeen years old because I was not prepared to focus on the things that were necessary for survival – food, clothing, and shelter. And for four years, the Air Force and the Amy provided food, clothing, and shelter. At times it was C-Rations for food, fatigues for clothing, and pup tents for shelter, but at least I didn't have to worry about those things while I served in the military. I did, however, have to concern myself with those basic needs for survival once I was discharged. So the basic things – food, clothing, and shelter were things I had to provide on my own. As I progressed through my various careers, the food, clothing, and shelter increased in quality and quantity. I'm sure I have more than I need, and I am not hungering for more. I can honestly say that the acquisition of "things" is not my focus, not my "main thing." I learned a long time ago that the accumulation of things did not bring me any more happiness. For some people, the pursuit of more things may be their main focus, and if it truly brings them happiness, then I salute them.

Besides a focus on one's self, or on personal achievements, or on the acquisition of more things as a primary focus on life, in other words the main thing in a person's life, is the focus on other people. When "the main thing" is enhancing relationships with other people and with making a difference in the lives of other people, we begin to live a life worth living. My wife and I are retired educators, so we are not rich by any stretch of the imagination. Primarily we live off of retirement and Social Security. But we are comfortable and really do not lack for anything we truly need. Over the years, the one thing that has brought me the most satisfaction is my relationships with other people. Virtually all of the jobs I have ever held required me to interact with other people. Teaching and coaching stand out the most for me because I interacted with students and athletes for fourteen years.

I last taught and coached over thirty years ago, but many of my former players still refer to me as "coach." I have wonderful memories of my interactions with students in the classroom and with athletes on the fields and on the court. I remember the students and the things they said and did more than I remember any "things" I may have gotten during those same years.

I believe memories have a more lasting impact on a person than the accumulation of things or even of personal achievements. A few years ago my wife and I decided that instead of exchanging gifts for Christmas, we would try to create memories. One Christmas we took a cruise. Another time we went to a University of North Carolina football Bowl game (we've done that three times). I remember the experiences of the cruise and the bowl games vividly and could not recall any "things" I received for Christmas during that same time period.

For each of us, deciding what the main thing is in our lives in the first step toward achieving the happiness for which we strive and overcoming the hurdles that get in the way of that goal.

Chapter 14: The Next Step

(Promise vs. Circumstance)

A few years ago, Chuck Pagano, then head coach of the Indianapolis Colts, had to take a leave of absence to deal with personal illness. At halftime of a game, a few months after taking the leave of absence, he showed up unannounced to talk to the team. His message was that his illness taught him to live in the promise not the circumstance and he wanted the team to play with that mindset. He wanted them to play with the promise of what they could attain instead of dwelling on whatever negative things were happening to the team.

The "promise" is what life could be. The "circumstance" is what life is at the present time. I liked what Coach Pagano said because I believe a hurdle to success and happiness is letting our circumstances keep us from realizing what our lives could be.

For Coach Pagano, the "promise" was to be healthy enough to attend the future weddings of his daughters. The "circumstance" was his battle with cancer. He told his players he could have allowed his "circumstance" (cancer) to keep him from looking to the possibilities life had to offer. Or, he said, he could look at the promise – attending future weddings – and live his life looking ahead and not wallowing in the circumstances of his life.

In order for us to understand the "promise," we must be honest with ourselves about our "circumstances." The "promise" is the goal at the finish line of the 100 meter dash vs. 100 meter hurdle analogy from Chapter 1. The "circumstances" are the hurdles that get in the way of reaching our goals. Most of this booklet is about identifying those hurdles and suggesting ways to overcome them.

In this chapter, I'm asking you to examine thoroughly the circumstance(s) that may be blocking your path to happiness. What is going on in your life right now that is keeping you from reaching your goals?

I started on this book over a year ago, and now, as I'm writing, our world is in the midst of the COVID-19 pandemic. For many people, this virus is a major "circumstance" that is keeping them from reaching their goals.

Many small businesses have either closed or been forced to lay off a number of employees. People without jobs are facing circumstances – hurdles – beyond their control.

The pandemic has also changed people's daily lives. Many venture outdoors only to go to the grocery store or to get gas. The isolation and boredom of staying inside for days on end creates the hurdle of depression.

To underscore Chuck Pagano's comments, most of us have allowed the circumstance of the pandemic to dictate how we live our lives. Thus, we are living in the circumstance and not in the promise.

I belong to two groups that are very important to me. The first is the Hickory Sunrise Rotary Club. We are a breakfast club that met every Wednesday morning at 7:00 a.m. on the campus of Lenoir-Rhyne University in Hickory, NC. The second group is the Foothills Veterans Helping Veterans. We are a group of men and women who want to help homeless and needy veterans in our area. We used to meet for fellowship Wednesday mornings at 10:00 a.m. at a local Panera Bread and would meet every Friday at 10:00 a.m. at the Hickory Soup Kitchen with needy veterans as we tried to see how we could help. The circumstance of the pandemic changed things for both groups. Lenoir-Rhyne University closed its doors to outside groups; Panera Bread closed its dining room; and the Soup Kitchen closed its doors as well. The Soup Kitchen continued to serve food, but they served it outdoors. No one could go inside. Both of the groups that were (are) special to me could not meet in person. Rotary projects were put on hold, and the veterans could no longer meet in person to discuss how to meet the needs of other veterans.

> The "promise" is what life could be. The "circumstance" is what life is at the present time.

I was the president of the Rotary Club when the pandemic began to alter people's lives. I communicated through email to keep the members up to date, but not seeing each other's faces and interacting with each other began to take its toll. The same was true for the veterans. At that point, we could have allowed the circumstance of the pandemic to keep both groups from reaching out to help others. We could have allowed our circumstance to be a hurdle preventing us from making a difference in the lives of other people.

Instead, we took some steps toward trying to realize the promise of what each group wanted to be. Welcome to Zoom!

I opened a Zoom account and contacted members of the Rotary club asking them to make sure they each had a Zoom account. Although our regular meetings were at 7:00 a.m., I wasn't confident the members would get up that early for a Zoom meeting. So, I scheduled the first one for 5:00 p.m. on a Wednesday. I had never used Zoom, much less hosted a meeting, but I felt we needed to make an effort to connect with each other. The virtual meeting was a huge success. We continued to meet virtually through the transition to new officers, and we still meet on Zoom. The new president is more daring than I because his virtual meetings are at 7:00 a.m. While the circumstances of the pandemic have limited our fund-raising and our service project efforts, we are still able to communicate, keep each other up-to-date with what is happening in our lives, and plan for the future. That planning is "living in the promise."

Once I realized virtual meetings could help people reconnect, I started hosting Zoom meetings for the veterans. Wednesdays had been the days we met for fellowship, and Fridays were the days we met to see how we could help veterans. In the virtual world, we changed that somewhat. I began hosting Zoom meetings on Wednesday mornings, and those meetings became our planning meetings. But more importantly, we were able to see each other and talk to each other. We were able to find out how each person and each family were doing. We were able to see how we could help each other during the difficult times of the pandemic. We saw how we could live in the promise and not in the circumstance.

We also found a way to meet in person. Downtown Hickory has an outdoor area designed for concerts and for relaxing while shopping or dining. It's called "Under the Sails" because of large white overhead coverings that look like sails on a ship. That area has tables and chairs and is open to the public. During one Zoom meeting we decided to try an in-person meeting Under the Sails. We agreed to wear masks and to socially distance ourselves. It worked beautifully. We now meet virtually every Wednesday and in person every Friday (weather permitting!). We are living in the promise, not the circumstance.

While it is essential for us to recognize the circumstances (hurdles) that impede the promise (goals) we want to achieve, it's equally important to continually revisit what the promise could be. As we journey along life's path, our goals often change. A goal of providing for a child's education could become, once that child has completed his or her education, a goal of saving for that long-awaited vacation you had been unable to take. Whether the goal has changed may or may not be impacted by your life's current circumstances. But understanding the goal and the hurdles will help you live in the promise and not in the circumstance.

Living in the promise means always striving to reach whatever goals you have set in life. Understanding the circumstances of your life will help you develop the steps necessary to live in the promise.

Chapter 15: Final Thoughts

My wife belongs to a "Book Club." I put those words in quotation marks because it is a club that reads but does not discuss the books they read. Each month they meet at a different person's house for lunch and fellowship and to exchange their books. But they don't talk about them.

One day Angela told me about a book she got during one of the club meetings from an author she didn't know, Louise Penny, and she thought I'd like the book. I'm into David Baldacci, Vince Flynn, and Lee Child. So I just smiled and went about my business. Angela got hooked on Louise Penny and began buying her books. She bought them all, and when Louise Penny came to Hickory, NC, Angela dragged me to the Patrick Beaver Library, a state-of-the-art facility in Hickory, so that Angela could meet and get a book signed by Louise Penny. When Louise signed the book, Angela said something to her. I was too far away to hear what she said, but it got the author's attention. Ms. Penny stood up and hugged Angela. When I saw that I got choked up because as I drew closer to the pair, I could hear Angela talking about losing a child to drugs. Obviously that resonated with Ms. Penny, but I didn't know why. I still didn't plan on reading her books, but I left the book signing with a deep admiration for Louise Penny.

A few months later, Angela received the latest Louise Penny book and again told me she thought I would like her books. We went to the beach, and I read the two books I had brought with me and suggested we go to Barnes & Noble and get a new book for me to read while I was basking on the beach. Again, Angela suggested I read the book she just finished. I told her I really didn't want to get into a "Mitford" type book – Angela kept talking about a little village called Three Pines, which I figured was the Canadian version of Mitford. She laughed and told me Louise Penny's books were mysteries and that I would really enjoy them. So, instead of going to Barnes & Noble, I took the book, went to the beach and began to read Louise Penny's latest novel. By the end of the first chapter, I was hooked.

When we returned from the beach trip, I told Angela I wanted to read more about Chief Inspector Armand Gamache, the lead character in the series. The book I read took place in Paris as Gamache and his wife, Reine-Marie, Canadian citizens, were visiting their children. There was a brief mention of Three Pines, the village in Canada, but I had no reference point for the village and the people in it. Angela said I should start with the first book in the series, which I did. Within four weeks I had read all sixteen books, including the most recent one again. I fell in love with the village of Three Pines and all of the quirky characters that live there. I learned also that Louise Penny had a substance abuse problem many years ago, so she could relate to what our son went through, hence the big hug she gave Angela.

I mention Ms. Penny's books about Chief Inspector Gamache because of something Gamache would always tell new recruits to the Surete' de Quebec, the provincial police force of Quebec. He would say, "There are four things that lead to wisdom. They are sentences we learn to say and mean. *I don't know. I need help. I'm sorry. I was wrong.*" - *Still Life* by Louise Penny

I want to end this little book on overcoming hurdles in our lives by sharing a few thoughts on Chief Inspector Gamache's words because wisdom is key to being successful.

I don't know. For many people, that sentence is difficult to say. "I don't know" is often seen as a sign of weakness. Knowledge is power, and admitting to not knowing can be seen by some as lacking in power, and none of us wants to be seen as lacking in power.

But Gamache is wise enough to know that wisdom, not power, is the key to happiness and success. And it is very wise to admit when one doesn't have an answer to a question. The first time I said "I don't know" when a student asked me a question, I thought I would lose credibility with my students. In fact, just the opposite happened. The students saw me as a fallible but honest person, and I gained their respect.

We've all met the "know-it-all," that person who always has THE answer to any issue, question, or problem. It usually doesn't take long before we begin to tune out these folks realizing that they do not possess wisdom – just a lot of hot air!

I need help. This sentence has always been difficult for me to say aloud. Similar to "I don't know," saying "I need help" might make some people feel weak and powerless. Males, especially, have difficulty admitting we need help. I've tried to convince my wife when traveling that we weren't lost; we were just not where we wanted to be. That was my excuse for not asking for directions – thus admitting I was wrong and that I needed help!

But by not asking for help – or even admitting we need help – we often create hurdles to success. To need help is to be human, not weak. Waiting too long to ask for help or coping poorly with stress becomes a self-imposed hurdle. It is a hurdle we put there ourselves because we don't want to appear weak or because we have too much pride to admit we can't do everything by ourselves.

If we are troubled, for whatever reason, it's important to get help. Stubbornness has never been an asset in overcoming problems. What we often fail to realize is that we are generally surrounded by people who care about us, who love us, and who want to help. But if we never ask for help, those who care about us become mired in a feeling of helplessness. They want to help and often offer that help, but unless we admit we need help and ask for that help, we will continue struggling, looking for answers, looking for a way out of depression. I mentioned, in Chapter 2, about trying to attain the bottom rung on the ladder that leads out of the pit of depression. Admitting that we need help and asking for that help is reaching that bottom rung.

> Wisdom, not power, is the key to happiness and success.

I'm sorry. We all know people who absolutely cannot apologize for anything they have done. Small offenses often become huge grudges simply because an apology was never offered. Worse, though, are insincere apologies. I remember many instances – when I was an elementary school principal – of seeing teachers make students apologize to each other for having committed some misdeeds. Once the students complied, the teachers were satisfied. But it was easy to see the apologies were only offered to keep the students from getting into further trouble. The apologies lacked sincerity. Among young children, that lack of sincerity is usually no big deal. It's different, though, among adults. Adults know an insincere apology when they hear one, and such an apology does little to help whatever situation necessitated an apology.

Dr. Ann Buscho, a licensed clinical psychologist, in a blog posted in November 2019, outlined five steps to making an effective apology:

a) Take responsibility for what you did to offend and articulate it in specific terms;
b) Understand and articulate how the offense affected the other person or persons;

c) State clearly the line that was crossed;

d) Clearly express remorse or sorrow for your actions;

e) State what you will do to avoid reoffending, and, when appropriate, offer restitution.

As I reread each of these steps, I realized how essential it is for the offender to truly understand he (or she) is in the wrong and understands exactly how the other person has been hurt. That understanding should lead to a sincere apology. Dr. Buscho makes a point that the offender should avoid asking for forgiveness. Asking for forgiveness unintentionally puts a condition on the apology and focusses on the offender's needs and not on the person offended.

I was wrong. While we may think we are always right, we are not. A major hurdle to success and happiness is always having to prove we are right and the other person is wrong. I know I'm not the only man whose only goal in arguing with his wife was to prove to how right I was.

It takes a person who is secure in him or herself to admit to being wrong. That admittance is not a sign of weakness. Instead, it is a sign of maturity and growth (it gets us out of middle school!).

Learning how to say that we *don't know*, we may *need help*, we are *sorry*, and/or we were *wrong* makes getting over hurdles easier.

Everybody faces hurdles in their lives. However, we have choices. Do we allow the hurdles to keep us from our goals, keep us from finding happiness, keep us from success? Or, do we instead choose to find ways to overcome the hurdles and live lives we are meant to live?

The choice is ours.

Some final thoughts/sayings to help you over the hurdles:

- Believe in yourself
- For every pit of depression there is a ladder of hope to lead you out of the pit
- Concentrate on strengthening yourself first so that you will be able to help others
- If you build a wall around yourself to protect yourself, you are also creating a way to isolate yourself
- Don't allow a crutch to keep you from standing on your own two feet
- Use an anchor for strength, not to tie you down and keep you from reaching your goals
- Guilt is a self-inflicted wound; no one can make you feel guilty
- Be a thoroughbred, not a plow horse
- Remember YAHOO – You Always Have Other Options
- "The Wizard of Oz" reminds us that we have what we need to be successful within us at all times
- Surround yourself with positive people
- Grow up
- Maintain a focus on what you want out of life
- Live in the promise, not the circumstance
- Be mature enough to admit when you don't know, need help, are sorry, and are wrong
- Remember, life is short and "it is insane to waste a moment of a lifetime that lasts but a moment"
- Believe in yourself

Dr. Ric Vandett retired in 2009 from public education after serving three years as Superintendent of Hickory Public Schools, Hickory, NC.

During a thirty-four year career in education, he taught high school English and coached football and basketball. As an administrator, he served as a middle school assistant principal, elementary school principal, Director of Instruction, Assistant Superintendent, and Superintendent of Schools.

He earned a BS in English and an MA in Public School Administration from Appalachian State University, in Boone, NC. Ric also earned a Doctorate in Educational Administration from Columbia University in New York in 1998. He served as Director of the Southwest Education Alliance, a consortium of eleven school districts in southwest NC, retiring in 2017. He is a Certified Lay Speaker for the United Methodist Church and has served St. Luke's UMC in Hickory, NC, as a Lay Leader. He is a Rotarian and served as chairperson on the board of Exodus Homes.

Ric is a Vietnam veteran serving with both the First Air Cavalry and the First Infantry Division in 1965 and 1966. He served as Chair of the Foothills Veterans Stand Down Committee for seven years and is on the board of the Foothills Veterans Helping Veterans.

Ric is married to the former Angela McCombs from Creedmor, NC. They have 4 children, 12 grandchildren, and 2 great grandchildren.

Made in the USA
Columbia, SC
30 March 2021